AMERICAN COMPOSERS ON AMERICAN MUSIC

A SYMPOSIUM

Edited by Henry Cowell

WITH A NEW INTRODUCTION BY THE EDITOR

FREDERICK UNGAR
PUBLISHING CO.
NEW YORK

Introduction

The purpose of this symposium is to present the composer's own point of view concerning creative music in America.

Those who follow music recognize that there is an extraordinary development now in process in American composition; yet very little general information on the subject is available, and that which is to be had is contradictory. The reason knowledge concerning American composition is confused is that it comes exclusively from professional critics who are not themselves composers. They do not understand in the least what is taking place in either feeling or technique, but give out vague personal impressions which have little relation to the reality and which differ widely with each individual critic. This is quite irrespective of whether the reviews are favorable or depreciatory.

This work is an experiment unprecedented in musical history, that of obtaining critical estimates from composers who may not always have a polished literary style but who know their subject, instead of from reviewers who are clever with words but do not know the principles of composition.

A number of well-known American composers were asked to contribute articles reviewing each other's compositions seriously, fearlessly, and in detail, and also to give their own opinions as to how creative music should progress. The authors here are therefore limited exclusively to composers. Since they are the ones who really know, if anyone does, the directions that contemporary music is taking, it is hoped that a clearer concept may result from reading their contributions. The analysis of one composer's work by another who is working in the same general field should be both provocative and instructive. And to obtain a synthetic and sympathetic understanding of the aims of any particular composer, why not ask him to relate them himself? He knows more about his aims than anyone else! Such a sympathetic understanding on the part of music lovers is something greatly to be desired, and would result in far greater pleasure being obtained by them from contemporary music. The notion that criticism must be vitriolic and destructive in order to be intelligent and interesting is an utter absurdity fostered by professional word-jugglers.

Naturally, such a symposium cannot include a contribution from every American composer. There are too many. It cannot even include a contribution from every well-known composer or every "good" composer. Nor can it be guaranteed with certainty that every composer who does contribute is a "good" composer! Other criteria also were considered. Composers who were included had to be persons who could write intelligibly. While literary style is not here the paramount consideration, it must be admitted that some very talented composers have absolutely no ability to set down their ideas in words. The composer also had to be someone with a definite point of view, preferably an individual one. This led to inviting many progressive and "modern" composers to give statements, as they often have a refreshing new outlook. It would not be of interest for a composer in such a work to give an exposé of schoolbook harmony and counterpoint, which is not only already known, and dry, but which has no relation to the direction now being taken by American music. Some more conservative composers were found, however, who have distinctive views. Their contributions are to be found here. By no means was it the desire to present one aspect only; on the contrary, leaders of every recognized phase of development were asked to contribute, and the fact that they disagree adds stimulation. Definite views are here placed over against each other and thus give a better concept of the different trends now being followed in America. Special consideration was given to composers who are developing indigenous types of music, as they have more to do with America than those who follow European styles very closely. Another consideration is that only composers who are at least somewhat known are interesting for the music-loving public to read. The composers included are therefore among those who of all Americans are the most performed by important organizations. Several foreign-born composers who have become Americans are included, and their opinions form an interesting contrast to those of the others. It will be seen that this work makes no pretense of being complete. Many important composers have been left out. But it is felt that every significant tendency is included.

In many instances it was utterly impossible to obtain original new articles from certain composers, but through the courtesy of various periodicals, which are given credit in the proper place, articles by them have been reprinted.

An examination of the scant bibliography of American composition is of interest in placing the position of the present work. The most serious and comprehensive book is J. T. Howard's *Our American Music*. This is an exhaustive historical survey, and contains biographical notes on the best-known contemporaries but no criticism of their works.

It is an excellent encyclopedia. Then comes Claire Reis's *American Composers of Today,* which is literally a catalogue of American works and is a most-needed and excellent compilation; in it no comments on the works are given. Paul Rosenfeld's *An Hour with American Composers,* like his articles scattered through several other books, presents impressions of American music by a musically sensitive amateur. It is very interesting as a disclosure of Rosenfeld's feelings, but gives no clue as to the real nature of the music it discusses. He chooses examples here and there, and makes no attempt to cover any particular field. Popular American music and its history is charmingly and completely disclosed in Isaac Goldberg's *Tin Pan Alley.* Finally, *Tune in, America!* by D. G. Mason, presents the ultra-conservative attitude toward American music and does not deal with any composer who has the slightest inkling of indigenous American style.

Where it proved unfeasible to obtain articles about important Americans from other composers, I have filled in the gap by writing the necessary articles myself. Otherwise, of course, the opinions expressed by the authors here do not necessarily concur with mine.

American Composers on American Music is not only the one literary expression of different composers' views from composers themselves but is the only book from any source which attempts a survey of the present tendencies of American art-music.

H. C.

New York City
January 12, 1933

vi]

Introduction to the 1962 Edition

These articles were assembled at a time when few people were aware that opinion about the creative direction of twentieth-century music was already lively and richly diverse among composers in the Americas. Most professional critics still made a point of avoiding direct contact with composers (just as they avoided meeting performers) lest they be influenced by personal considerations, and our symphony programs were heavily weighted in favor of eighteenth- and nineteenth-century European music.

As a result, contemporary music, when it was played at all, was judged in accordance with nineteenth-century European standards, and the fresh attitudes and concepts that flooded musical composition in this hemisphere after World War I were far from being in general circulation. Many cultivated people still held the naive idea that in time one single musical style would develop to represent all of us, and there were one or two American composers in those days who agreed with them, and who were distressed to find themselves in the variegated company presented in this book.

I have never believed that any one individual could speak for an entire continent, in all its variety of cultures and societies. Nor has it ever seemed reasonable to me to believe that there could ever be one single "mainstream of music," except for some brief time in some small place. If Europe had really established such a "mainstream," how odd that the French and the Germans had come to no agreement about where it was to be found! In any case it seemed to me even then that to be American was to honor difference, and to welcome the experimental, the fresh and the new, instead of trying to establish in advance the road our creative life should follow.

So I thought that American music could best be demonstrated to the general reader by asking composers of widely divergent views to write about whatever they found sympathetic in one another, pairing author and subject in as provocative and illuminating a way as I could. In some cases I reprinted earlier articles, and where cooperation proved difficult or dilatory, I wrote the articles myself in order to maintain the original broadly representative intention. No attempt was made to include every individual then writing music, but rather to demonstrate the wide range of aims and ideas then current by choosing for discussion those composers who seemed most effectively to illustrate them. Of course, I had to depend upon composers who had already demonstrated their ability to use words intelligibly. Some of these men preferred not to write about other composers, but were willing to write on some general aspect of the creative scene.

From the point of view of 1961, of course, the omission of several important subsequent developments leaps to the eye: contemporary American opera was then in its infancy; influences from the classical and folk musics of the Orient were of little interest to anyone but myself, and Charles Seeger's insistence that American composers should listen to their own country music, to the various sorts that had circulated on this continent for two hundred to three hundred years, began to be effective only after about 1935. The several personal styles developed by atonalists in the two Americas were ten years or so away. Schoenberg, Stravinsky, Bartok and Hindemith had not yet moved to the United States.

However, when the reprinting of this symposium was suggested to me, I reread the book for the first time in nearly thirty years and was pleasantly surprised to find that I seem to have placed my bets well, since so many of today's major figures in American music had found a place in the volume then. Half a dozen of these men have consistently maintained a position of leadership in one "school" or another, having in the last thirty years broadened the scope of their music and significantly developed it. And most of the other names discussed or listed here would still have to be included in any similar attempt to present the many facets of American music today, though it is, of course, true that two or three of them would be known only to a rather specialized musical public.

If I were undertaking a book like this today, I would undoubtedly be less brash about it, and this is probably equally true of others who wrote for the volume between 1929 and 1932. But I have not felt that the book's character should be watered down by the mild afterthoughts of "mature consideration." It was expected from the beginning to reveal as much about its authors as it did about their subjects, and if today this seems to be even more true than I anticipated, it can't be helped. Except for three misspelled proper names and two footnotes, nothing has been changed or added.

The articles simply present a survey of American fine-art music, gathered together in a spirit of welcome to variety, and written during a period of great creative activity in music in the Americas by some of the people who were writing that music. We were no less enthusiastic, partisan and critical than young men are now. Moreover, our self-confidence had just been given notable support by famous critics in Europe, following the presentation, by the Pan-American Association of Composers, of a series of all-American programs played by the leading orchestras in several European capital cities in 1931 and 1932. It was at this time that one began to find expressed in European journals the recognition that we in this hemisphere had a solid group of composers who had achieved skill equal to that of Europeans in the use of the current twentieth-century European techniques. Even more European interest had been generated by the discovery that the Americas also had several composers who wrote with authority in styles and techniques that owed little to any but a purely American experience of sound. This European recognition was of major importance in the long struggle to persuade orchestras here to give a hearing to American music, at a time when players and conductors were still trained almost entirely abroad.

It has, of course, taken a long time for the composers who felt impelled to compose outside the old traditions of Europe to achieve the solid ground of wide recognition in their own country. Today, however, there is no question but that those who were most determined and uninhibited in their "experimentalism," and who seemed so shockingly untamed in the Twenties, are now widely thought of as representing the "essence" of America.

As to this I should like to repeat here the concluding paragraph of my introductory chapter to this book, written in January, 1933:

> "American composition up to now has been tied to the apron-strings of European tradition. To attain musical independence, more national consciousness is a present necessity for American composers. The results of such an awakening should be the creation of works capable of being accorded international standing. When this has been accomplished, self-conscious nationalism will no longer be necessary."

HENRY COWELL

Shady, New York
November 24, 1961

Acknowledgments

Previously published articles appearing here through the kind permission of publishers and authors include:

"Carl Ruggles," by Charles Seeger, by permission of *The Musical Quarterly*.

"Edgar Varèse," by Henry Cowell, by permission of *Modern Music*.

"Aaron Copland up to Now," by Theodore Chandler, by permission of *The Hound and Horn*.

"Roy Harris, An American Composer," by Henry Cowell, by permission of *The Sackbut*.

"Carlos Chávez—Mexican Composer," by Aaron Copland, by permission of *The New Republic*.

"Charles Seeger," by Henry Cowell, by permission of *The Fortnightly*.

"Charles Ives," by Henry Cowell, by permission of *Modern Music*.

"Some Problems of the American Composer," by Roy Harris, by permission of *Scribner's*.

"The Music of Mexico," by Carlos Chávez, by permission of the Society for Cultural Relations with Latin America.

"Music and Its Future," by Charles Ives, by permission of *New Music Quarterly*.

Contents

COMPOSERS IN REVIEW OF
OTHER COMPOSERS

Trends in American Music

Before reading the opinions of
a number of different composers with diversified ideas, it will
be well to examine various tendencies in contemporary American music and to obtain a general notion of the grouping of
composers according to accomplishments and ideals. It is
obviously impossible to classify them exactly. All of them
to some extent transcend the narrowing limits of pigeonholes
or schools. Many write at one time in one way, at another
time in another way. With European composers it is often
possible to say with a fair degree of accuracy that they are
"expressionists" or "impressionists," or that they are "atonalists" or "polytonalists," et cetera. With American composers
these terms practically never apply, for nearly all Americans
have mixtures of such elements in their music.

If it is understood, therefore, that the categories are very
general and not to be regarded too definitely, we can make
some groupings based on examination of the music of American composers.

One group is of Americans who have developed indigenous materials or are specially interested in expressing some
phase of the American spirit in their works. To this group
belong: Charles Ives, who started with a foundation of
Yankee folk-music and built himself a whole new realm of
musical resources to keep the true spirit of it in his art-
music; Carl Ruggles, who independently and painstakingly
worked out the system in which he composes little by little,
and with very scant outside influence, in his Vermont home

(that his style seems a bit Schoenbergian is more an accident of coincidence than a genuine Schoenberg influence); Charles Seeger, who was one of the first in America to experiment with independent materials; Roy Harris, who makes researches into new forms with a special view as to whether or not they express an American feeling, although his works are in most respects conservative; Henry Brant, Canadian, who has invented a new concept of harmony and some other individual ideas; Ruth Crawford, who is very constructive and is working on new aspects of melodic form and other musical resources.

I (Henry Cowell) belong to this group also, as I have initiated independently various new sorts of harmony, rhythm, counterpoint, and other musical mediums. Colin McPhee, Canadian, follows to some extent the modern French style of clever music but treats it in a personal manner. His music forms a sort of bridge between the more characteristic Americans and those who are somewhat Europeanized. Carlos Chávez, Mexican, and Alejandro Caturla and Amadeo Roldan, Cubans, take native musical material from the people of their lands and have in each case built a somewhat independent cultivated style, which retains the original spirit. Modern French music has been a powerful influence in all three cases, however.

A second group is of foreign-born composers who have made America their home, and who have developed indigenous tendencies in their works. To this group belongs Leo Ornstein, Russian, who startled the world with his unheard-of discords and his renunciations of form. He developed his style in America about 1915. His work is not treated in detail here because it has not influenced the general trend since

1920 at the latest, and because since about 1920 his style has become more and more conventional until it can no longer be considered original.

Also Edgar Varèse, French, who has explored new possibilities of percussion sounds, and also created many other new orchestral effects; Dane Rudhyar, French, who has created new tonal alchemies and has developed a philosophy which necessitates a musical system of its own; Carlos Salzedo, Basque-French, who has found some hundreds of new possible sounds on a harp; Nicolas Slonimsky, Russian, who has invented a musical scheme built on the use of concords made modern by cross-relations; Joseph Schillinger, Russian, who has applied himself to creating a style specially suited for electrical instruments and has invented a composing machine for creating music in any style, old or new!

A third group consists of Americans who are in many respects original but who are influenced by modern Teutonic music. Belonging to this group are: Adolph Weiss, who has utilized a Schoenbergian idiom to express his outlook on life which is quite different from Schoenberg's and is philosophically American; Wallingford Riegger, who uses atonality to produce well-formed works with humor and a long-continued melodic line; John J. Becker, who attempts to recreate the spirit of ancient church music through the use of modern atonal polyphony; Gerald Strang, who takes a device, such as inversion, and constructs whole compositions without departing from it; Richard Donovan, who mixes impressionistic harmony into an atonal fabric.

A fourth group is of Americans who also are often somewhat original but who follow either modern French or "neoclassical" tendencies. To this group belong: Roger Sessions, who creates serious music in which influences from many composers and countries are to be found but which is particularly close to the modern French; George Antheil, who has sensationalized each new Parisian development, including Stravinsky's various phases, and has now turned neo-classical in the *Gebrauchsmusik* direction; Marc Blitzstein, whose contribution to music is not in new sounds but in sudden pauses, and who has turned from following Schoenberg to following the current French tendency; Henry Eichheim, who superimposes Oriental instruments and impressions upon a conventional French style; Marion Bauer, whose works are in an impressionistic-modern vein; Virgil Thomson, who combines neo-classicism with the modern French idea that superficial amusement is profoundly philosophical.

George Antheil occupies a unique position among American composers, since he has the reputation of being the most radical. Also, he was the first radical American to be much spoken of and performed in Europe. His claim on America is very slight. He was born of Polish parents (in Trenton, New Jersey, in 1900) and moved to Europe before he was full grown. He has lived there ever since, with the exception of a few months in America as a visitor. Also one must say that his music is very evidently European. He has been much with Stravinsky, and the most famous epoch of his music (the period of the "Ballet Mécanique") consists of a mixture of literal fragments from Stravinsky together with sensational but not strictly musical additions, such as scoring in the "Ballet Mécanique" for Liberty motors and a raft of mechanical pianos. It is on such sensationalisms, however, that Antheil's reputation as a devilish radical is built. Real originality in the music itself is not to be found in the very period of his writing that became famous for its radicalism! The reputation was obtained because Antheil's real talent is in discovering very quickly what the latest trend is, and imitating it immediately, exaggerating it if possible. In more recent years Antheil has followed successively "neo-classicism" and *Gebrauchsmusik* very closely after their instigators. Yet in Antheil's recent works there is more real originality than in the showier early works. His new works, such as the chamber concerts for eight instruments, show an attempt to wrestle with the more fundamental problems of melody and counterpoint, and to create serious and lasting values. In this attempt he is often crude. But it is the direction that counts. With his undoubtedly unusual if not great talent, he will eventually be able to weed out mere technical rawness, now that he has decided to try really to say something worth saying. His older and more famous way was to take the latest word and dish it up in such a way as to dazzle and to create immediate interest, but with utter superficiality. The idea was to amuse Paris for a day—never to consider lasting values. This is hardly Antheil's fault, for why should a composer consider lasting values when he knows that in the great cities, though a first performance may possibly be obtained, a second performance is considered boresome and can never be had? Lasting values are of importance in a work only if it is to have re-performances. Antheil today, however, does not write to please and amuse a small clique of the supercilious sophisticated but has taken the finer course of trying to attain genuine musicality. Others, who have followed this ideal longer, are now farther advanced in its practice than Antheil. But with his native gifts and shrewd views he may yet outrun those in the lead! His older style pleases neither Antheil himself nor any serious musician or music-lover. Antheil's newer style is as yet little known, but should be vastly interesting to follow. It has little reference to his fantastic past, in which he was the naughty boy of American composers.

A fifth group may be made of Americans who do not attempt to develop original ideas or materials but who take those which they already find in America and adapt them to a European style. To this group belong: Aaron Copland, who uses jazz themes and rhythms in music which is otherwise modern French in conception. Such of his music as does not utilize jazz material is also French in style, and is of the type that is amusing and sounds well immediately; George Gershwin, who is the greatest master of real jazz but who extracts all original qualities from his jazz and puts it into a typically European sentimental style, mixing Liszt, Puccini, Stravinsky, and Wagner when he tries to write "classical" music; John Alden Carpenter, who uses American titles, and sometimes traces of Negro themes, in a style taken direct from France; Werner Janssen, who also uses American titles so as to be considered American in his music but whose hodgepodge style stems from the French; Bernard Rogers, who mixes popular with serious music in a pseudo-French style, with American impressionistic titles; Frederick Jacobi, who adapts American Indian themes to a semi-modern European orchestral idiom; Frederick Converse, who, like Janssen, writes basically French music under American titles, although his music sounds very different from Janssen's.

To this group also belong two foreign-born Americans: Ernest Bloch and Louis Gruenberg. Ernest Bloch, Swiss, composes well-formed post-Wagnerian music based on a combination of Teutonic orchestral forms with Hebrew-type thematic material. His composition called "America" is exactly in this same style in spite of the American folk-tunes he used in it, which he had to alter to fit his European taste. Louis Gruenberg, Russian, has taken jazz themes and treated them in familiar Central-European fashion. Many Europeans who never visited America, such as Krenek and Haba, even Hindemith and Stravinsky, have made similar arrangements of jazz. Gruenberg's version, however, possesses an original humor and deft orchestration.

A sixth group can be made of Americans who work along more or less conservative lines and make no attempt to write anything departing from general types of European music. There are a large number of these. Howard Hanson, Arthur Shepherd, Arnold Bennett, Arthur Farwell, Theodore Chandler, John Beach, Edward B. Hill, Wesley LaViolette, Randall Thompson, Emerson Whithorne, Walter Piston, Leo Sowerby, and Deems Taylor are typical examples of some who are frequently presented. There are many differences among them and many points of interest in their music, but since they do not possess any qualities distinguishing them as especially American in their work it is out of place to treat of them here. Howard Hanson, however, might perhaps be placed in group one, since, although his music contains nothing which does not come from European sources, he has done more than almost any other person to foster productions of American composers of all tendencies.

A seventh group may be made of foreign-born Americans who continue to compose in European fashion. They make no pretense of trying to be American but retain their original style. Charles Martin Loeffler, Vladimir Dukelsky, Lazare Saminsky, Nicolai Berezowsky, Joseph Achron, Isador Freed, Bernard Waganaar, and Tadeuz Jareci belong to this class. Both of the last two groups might be lengthened almost indefinitely.

An eighth group might be made of young composers who give promise of developing originally and becoming independently American. Henry Brant, one of the youngest, I have mentioned before, as he has already made original contributions to American musical literature. Vivian Fine is vigorous and radical, with a bristlingly harsh and discordant style. Her technique is rapidly improving, and she has already produced works which have commanded a hearing in important organizations abroad. Lahn Adohmyan, a young Russian-American, is also well worth watching. His music is modern but plain, with conscious crudity and primitivity carried out artistically for the purpose of expressing proletariat ideals. Jerome Moross is a vigorous experimenter, and is not afraid to go as far as his imagination can carry him in exploring new orchestral sounds, slides, and rhythms. He is not much interested in melodic contour or counterpoint, but rather in sound itself, and the rhythm of sounds reiterated or periodically changed. Bernard Hermann is also an experimenter, but in the direction of making the orchestra into a more satisfactory medium for polyphony, in which he is primarily interested as a composition medium. He attempts varied melodic line and long flowing curves of counterpoint. He drives his orchestra into narrowed channels of reinforced unisons to bring out these curves. J. Lehman Engel also makes dissonant counterpoint his main mode of expression; but, whereas with Hermann the materials are the main interest, with Engel the thing to be expressed is paramount. Engel weaves the human voice into his instrumental lines, and often writes upon semi-mystical subjects. His counterpoint is more short-lined than Hermann's, but within its shorter line is more perfected in detail. William Russell is developing a music of percussion only. Elie Seigmeister, Evelyn Berckman, Israel Citkowitz, and Irwin Heilner are working along more conservative lines but are growing in breadth and mode of expression.

Without creating any more of these rather arbitrary divisions, one may mention Hans Barth, Dutch-American, who composes for quarter-tones, and Julian Carrillo, Mexican, who composes for quarter-tones and other intervals finer than a half-step. Neither of these men can be considered a composer. Their music is meant to illustrate a system and serves its purpose. Other than as illustration, it has no importance.

There are also two interesting individual cases which are difficult to group:

William Grant Still, Negro, uses his people's themes and feelings as a base for his music, which is otherwise in modern style with some rather vague European influence. Perhaps he possesses the beginnings of a genuine new style. At present, however, his works are unformed and contain many crudities. Only later developments will show whether or not his present promise will be fulfilled. T. Carl Whitmer is an American who has been very independent, separated from all influences from abroad, and who, like Ives, has spent many years in creating serious music which expresses his delicate and poetic approach toward life and reality. But while in the case of Ives this process has resulted in the formation of an unprecedented and well-rounded style, in the case of Whitmer it has resulted in a style that seems utterly conventional on first hearing and resembles that of many religious organist-composers. That which gives his music real power and originality in feeling rather than in sound content is that, although the style proves to be conservative, he came to it through his own experiments. It is not a style which he borrowed from somewhere else. He is the most independent composer we have among those whose music sounds conservative.

All the foregoing categories include men of great value, and valuable music can be written in any of the ways they represent. It is particularly not my desire to criticize adversely composers who follow European standards. It would be absurd to expect that Europeans should change their musical style suddenly because of moving to America. Some of the most talented composers we have are those like Weiss, who follow modern Teutonic principles, or who, like Copland, follow modern French modes. The surprising fact is, however, that we have also produced some genuinely indigenous additions to music. Most of our composers have not yet begun to utilize these additions nor to add to them; some of the more independent ones, however, do utilize or invent such additions. In any case, it is of interest to clarify the issue whether certain music is American in essence or only through its title or the chance nationality of the composer.

Certain music may be called essentially American because it expresses some phase of American life or feeling. Other music may be named American if it contains new materials which are created by an American composer or the American folk.

Nationalism in music has no purpose as an aim in itself. Music happily transcends political and racial boundaries and is good or bad irrespective of the nation in which it was composed. Independence, however, is stronger than imitation. In the hands of great men independence may result in products of permanent value. Imitation cannot be expected to produce such significant achievements.

American composition up to now has been tied to the apron-strings of European tradition. To attain musical independence, more national consciousness is a present necessity for American composers. The result of such an awakening should be the creation of works capable of being accorded international standing. When this has been accomplished, self-conscious nationalism will no longer be necessary.

Carl Ruggles

At the present time (March 1932) any critical study of Carl Ruggles and his work must proceed under this handicap—that the "Sun-Treader," *magnum opus* of his mature period, which received its première in Paris on February 25, 1932, has not yet been performed in New York and hence cannot be considered except in so far as a pencil score, rather difficult to read, has been shown to friends. This leaves for examination a comparatively small body of material; small, considering its recognized importance, and mostly composed between the years 1918 and 1926,* viz.: "Toys," for voice and orchestra, vocal score published in 1922 by H. W. Gray; "Angels," for six muted trumpets, published in 1925 by Curwen & Son; "Three Songs with Orchestra," in manuscript; "Men and Mountains," for small orchestra, published in 1928 by *New Music;* "Portals," for thirteen strings, published in 1930 by *New Music.*

To understand how such a minimum of output can have raised its composer to his acknowledged eminence demands a consideration of three elements: the man, his times, and his work—its technical as well as its critical make-up. Such consideration should be unbiased, of course; but that is practically impossible, because all three of these elements act too forcefully to put one either in the camp of rooters-for or hooters-against. Next best is frank bias, clearly ex-

---

* It is generally understood that all work composed previous to 1918 has been destroyed or its publication and performance denied by its composer.

pressed and open to correction by any intelligent reader. Therefore let it be understood that the present undertaking frankly admits a friendship of over ten years' standing, a quite unusual kinship of taste in artistic matters, and an almost blood-brotherhood—for, without a doubt, common ancestors burned witches with uncommon fury.

To begin with the man, an astonishingly large and heterogeneous group of friends will unhesitatingly dub Carl Ruggles the most delightful character in contemporary American life. The very quintessence of New-Englandism, he mixes with any crowd, but not in the fashion of the man who is lost in or takes over the character of the crowd. Not Carl! He stands out among his fellows as readily in a concert audience or a well-dressed party as at the corner store in Arlington, Vermont. He is just as likely to be having for dinner the local traffic cop or the village house-painter as a distinguished writer, artist, capitalist, or scientist the night you appear, without prior notice, at the converted schoolhouse that gives him a music-room forty feet square and twenty feet high.

He is an excellent *raconteur*. He can tell stories to a mixed party that few would dare to tell in the proverbial smoking-room full of commercial travelers. He can paint better than many professional painters, can mend antique furniture, and can criticize anything. He is one of those rare people who have a generalized artistic taste. It is a narrow taste, very particular, and quite of the absolutist type, with no gradations. His perception is of "the real thing" or nothing, almost as quick and positive in a craft as in an art. But if the thing is not of the particular type he approves, it is "rotten," and a well-fortified vocabulary and a handy delivery are quick on the trigger.

Perhaps it is this clearness of view and the joy in expressing it that makes its undoubted strength also his one great weakness, socially speaking, that is. The keenness of his admiration or aversion, not only for works of art but for men who have or have not the quality which is his *sine qua non,* causes him to be over-enthusiastic or over-condemnatory. For instance, the scientist, the artist, the village contemporary who is present either corporeally or to Carl's mind is *the* finest scientist, artist, good fellow—or the worst. If the best, naturally, the praised man warms to Carl's attitude. He seems to become what he is felt to be. Naturally, too, the feeling is reciprocated, so that it is very difficult when with Carl not to be two gods legislating for the universe that lies tremblingly awaiting verdict after verdict. Later, when the universe gets in its say, one is likely to become a bit ashamed of oneself, of the legislative activity, and even of Carl. But at the next meeting Olympus looms and compunctions vanish.

This sounds strange to lots of people. But they forget that such procedure is the very essence of the artistic method. It is the poet, primarily, who puts everything and everybody in place. And why? Because "he knows best—and knows he knows it!" Similarly, in music, the composer who really *is* a composer puts tones and rhythms in their place, and whether or not the people agree the people have to and do come around. There were at least two examples of artistic arrogance among the composers of the last century. Like them, Ruggles is a short man with tall ideas; and, like them, he has spurned the academicians, who, as before, have claimed there was some slip, some gap in the chain that led from the *assumption* of godship (as claimed above, a legitimate assumption for any artist) to the recognition of it by other men. In the case of Ruggles some people have remained incredulous on account of the small amount of his work; others charge a technical obscurantism. The argument advanced here is that all these things are contributory but there are others more basic, and all the rest of us are subordinate to them—so it is not Carl's fault if he is too. The problem, so far as it has been developed here, then, consists largely in its more elaborate statement. To put it first very hypothetically, here is a man who has an unusual number of the attributes of genius: might it not be that if he had been born at another time or in a different place he would have been able to make his grandiose dreams more palpable and to turn out a bulk of work that would compel the acceptance of his notions of beauty as the standard of his day and fix him in the honored position of the first great musician of an epoch? Of all the men past or present in American music, who has come nearer to filling this hypothetical position?

The placing of Carl Ruggles in this position makes the consideration of him and his work not merely that of one man and his doings, but rather of what one might more accurately call the tragedy of American music. To comfort the conservatives let it be said that here is no musical Anti-Christ screaming sensationally after strange gods. Quite the opposite. To Carl Ruggles, there are not different kinds of beauty: there is only one kind, and that he prefers to call the "sublime." What he wants to see in music is that quality which makes him steadfastly call Händel and Bach the greatest composers. He merely tries to achieve it in a different way. No music, he believes, can be great that does not have it.

In studies of personality, psychological, literary, or otherwise, some accounting has been given of this distinct type of artistic effort—the attempt to convey the most approved ideal by the least approved means. It has not been of uncommon occurrence at other times, in other places. The tragedy of American music is that it has never occurred in America. But, Jehovah-complex, substitute activity, whatever music is to Carl Ruggles, he is a natural-born musician and seems to have been since the days when, a *Wunderkind* in a velvet suit, he was put up to play his fiddle for President Grover Cleveland—of all people!

Why—again of all people—should a Cape Cod Yankee boy, of distinguished ancestry but an upbringing full of hardship, renounce his inheritance of the whaleman's sea-going business instinct and cultivate the musical style of two respectable burghers who lived in northern Germany two hundred years ago? Could it have been an economic determinism that impelled him to Harvard, where, as an irregular, he outdid the intellectual snobbery of Holden Chapel and Symphony Hall? Was it the latest development of the frontier spirit that called him to Winona, Minnesota, to take a brilliant post in a conservatory whose chief asset was a catalogue, so that he was forced to shift for himself, to conduct poorly subsidized opera and symphony concerts, and so to become filled with the idea that "Versunkene Glocke" (in English) would be a nice opera to write in New York? With most of the composers in America being smug and conventional, quite content to let the current confusion of great utterance and post-Wagnerian rhetoric remain undisturbed, why should one man (maybe there have been others—but God help them, where are they?) endure poverty and humiliation in devotion to the entirely unremunerative task of distinguishing between them and attempting the formulation of a technique for makers, rather than remakers, of music?

Psychology and other sciences may have much to contribute to the answer. But it would be a lengthy one and no musician would read it. The fact is the life of Carl Ruggles is a logical implication of American music. Whether he or another lived it, makes not so very much difference—except to Carl and his friends. The rôle was there to play. Someone had to play it: someone would want to play it. Now it is being played. And the least we can do is to give homage to the tenacious courage that has at last found a considerable degree of peace on earth as the sage of Arlington, Vermont.

As homage I think the best we can do is to try to understand his times, the current state of affairs that puts a perfectly good genius in a place where it is so difficult for him to function. Of course, "Carl is lazy." To achieve the suitable state of mind, he requires an uproarious breakfast, after which he starts to work and works, ordinarily, until time for lunch. Sometimes he keeps going all day, but he keeps changing what he has written—nothing is so difficult as to resist doctoring this or that. Of course no orchestra is big enough: parts just naturally clamor unceasingly for extra horns and clarinets. Then again, there are only twelve semitones per octave, and everyone knows that is a pitiful number, especially when you have only eight octaves and, at least theoretically, no melody may repeat a given tone until at least nine or ten others have intervened. Furthermore, a melody starts way down in the bass and ascends: first thing you know it has reached a height where the characteristic tone-quality desired cannot be maintained—the first string of the 'cello can go only so far. Substitute after substitute, the limits of the gamut are there and the melody is still full of energy to soar. Or perhaps a fine resounding chord, *fortississimo*, with about ten different constituents, simply must follow while all eight horns are ripping out a line in unison—there are not enough instruments in any orchestra in the country. And so on. Is it the composer's fault?

In Europe the same wants are felt. But there if a man does not quickly learn to forget them and to confine himself to the use of the means available he is not "routined," not *grundlich*, and the reproach is usually sufficient to put him in his place. In America, on the other hand, one can get by without the reproach being much felt. What is conventional is perhaps more generally done here than in Europe; but the opportunity to contemplate the unconventional in the full panoply of its latent possibilities is actually more real, more present, in America, even more practical. Europe is such a slave to its musical past that it is almost impossible for it even to imagine the tyranny it suffers under. Something new in music? Fifteen years have gone by without one even childlike effort at anything new. And now, we hear, it's modern to be conventional! To be exact, some new handling in respect to pitch has been discovered and worked with, as in Schoenberg's twelve-tone scheme. But in dynamics, tone-quality, tempo, accent, and rhythm in general, as in melody, counterpoint, and even harmony, not to mention form, European music has remained consistently war, if not pre-war, and shows every sign of continuing to do so. Neo-classicism? Say, rather, pseudo-romanticism or neo-rococo.

Of course, from a historical point of view, fifteen years is not much time. But it is a lot of time to a man at the height of his career. A lot of time and a determining time: time to use a technique or to adapt one, if not too much changing is involved. But the only technique is the somewhat second-hand European one. That, as has already been pointed out, is so inadequate that one spends all one's time trying to patch it here and supplement it there, and there is not much time left for finishing things. Most people don't even sense this; but Ruggles knows it well. That, I think, is the reason why the "Sun-Treader" was on the ways for six years, most of that time a pile of enormous sheets of paper—sheets some twenty feet long, so that a double-triple canon of 39 measures could be viewed all at once in the consideration of the cancrizans.

There may be men in Europe who have found themselves in the same predicament. One can only wish they would speak up. Have their more facile contemporaries merely smothered them in a smoke-screen of opportunism?

In America there are only a few composers of any kind, yet even with this minimum of competition, with the possibilities clear in sight, and with the money here to pay for the realization of the possibilities, still the hide-bound conventionality of professional life and patronage alike withholds even a cent for the building of the new, while millions of dollars go into the rebuilding of the old. There are a thousand things we could do for music. But how many care for that? There must be more players, more players, whether or not they have a living art to play.

Of course, music may continue in Europe for a long time along the lines of custom, with mild experiment on the traditions inherited from the forefathers. But in America there are practically no traditions because there were no forefathers, that is, musical ones—they were all out chopping trees and killing Indians. So that now, when the art of music is trying to make up three centuries of lost time, it is doubly a shame that not only Europe must stew in its own juice but America, also, in that same juice. Now is the very time when a daring departure saving centuries of slow development could be made. We need a complete gamut for every known orchestral tone-color and for many still unknown but certainly there. We need at least a start toward the development of a tonal system using smaller intervals than the semi-tone. We need thorough familiarity with the musics of the great Oriental civilizations, and these musics, so fast dying, must be recorded soon or they will vanish and become regretted by our more enlightened descendants as we regret the loss of the Library of Alexandria. We need an accurate notation to replace the clumsy symbolism now in use. We need a revision of our music-education materials and methods so that the young music will not be perverted and befuddled as it now is by its well-meaning, costly, but thoroughly inept instruction—always looking backward, never forward. And, above all, we need a revision of the whole attitude toward music—that attitude which *says* nice things about the rôle of music in society but actually *puts* it to uses as base as ever in the history of man.

The tragedy of American music is that it has this opportunity for a short time before the imitation of European gods descends upon us and fixes us in a traffic of ten miles an hour—a stale neo-Romanism. We can go sixty—we have the brains, the money, and the opportunity. But the bringing of them together is not happening. Of course, Carl Ruggles thinks dimly of this. He has, thanks to the faith of an enlightened patron, a living free to work patiently and with a large degree of happiness toward the achievement of each particular problem that presents itself to him. Since the breaking up of the International Composers' Guild, he has lacked a demand, a need, for his work. Edgar Varèse was the only man that could make Carl produce one work a year. There is some sense in the *Gebrauchsmusik* idea! But Henry Cowell has stepped boldly into the breach; so we may expect an increased output from our musical ancient mariner.

It now remains to sketch the nature of the technical and critical problem that Ruggles' work embodies.

The fundamental critical desideratum has been stated, namely, the achievement of the grandeur, the complete convincingness, the sublimity that inheres in the best work of Bach and Händel—for instance, in the slow movement of the double concerto, the D minor Toccata, *"Ombra mai fu,"* and can still be seen in the *Fifth Symphony* of Beethoven, the *Unfinished* of Schubert, and some other later works (but not of Schumann, Liszt, Grieg, or Tschaikowsky). The technical means by which the material of an art which has in recent years drifted so far from such an ideal is to be re-induced to its service is interesting and involves critical determinations throughout the process. To Ruggles, the sustained melodic line is of prime importance. In the earlier work, the fabric is frankly homophonic—in "Angels," for instance—but by the time "Portals" is written, a contrapuntal rigor almost conceals the basically chordal conception. Such passages as have been seen of the "Sun-Treader" reveal a still more contrapuntal structure; practically, counterpoint has challenged the chordal origins of the technique.

The determining feature or principle of the melodic line

is that of non-repetition of tone (either the same tone or any octave of it) until the tenth progression. This applies rigidly to the leading melody and characterizes the other parts to a surprising extent, though in "Portals" many repeated notes can be found at the fourth, fifth, and sixth progression.

It would indeed be a great surprise to most musicians and music-lovers to realize what a sensitiveness has been developed by adherence to this principle. The offense felt by a false repetition depends to a large extent upon the context and the handling of the intervening tones as well as upon their number. The present writer feels that repetition can be made, provided it is skilfully done, at rare instances as soon as the fourth progression, though normally it can only be done easily at the sixth or seventh. Ruggles is becoming more and more convinced that it cannot ordinarily be done sooner than the ninth or tenth, and he has developed a sensitiveness that is uncanny. The reader must understand that this avoidance of the repeated tone is not, with him, to any great extent an intellectual feat. Not given to analysis and remarkably free of what is ordinarily referred to as the "theory" of music (that is, the verbal description of the *practice* of the masters of the preceding century), he will often tell you a melody or melodic line is bad and will point out the place where it is bad, only later discovering that it is on account of a false repetition. Reiteration (immediate repetition) is occasionally effective, but only occasionally. The repetition of tones resulting from reiteration of phrase (as in the sixth and seventh measures of "Portals" and again in the ninth and tenth) constitutes, I believe, almost the only exception to the principle. The way a melody, corrected for its repeated tones, appears "cleaned up," purged of some taint difficult to describe, is a startling thing to contemplate. The "false tone" appears, in an otherwise well-made line, as a hole in a fine fabric—it almost calls out for mending!

The theoretical statement of this principle, its historical grounding, and its implications have not been hitherto ventured into. There can be no doubt that repetition and, especially, reiteration of tone have been overdone by some modern composers, particularly by those of the Impressionist persuasion. A strand with many repeated tones is very likely to exhibit functional weaknesses, that is to say, a lack of melodic momentum, a progress that depends too much upon mere lapse of time or a "railroad" rhythm and not enough upon tendencies inherent in the tonal and rhythmic forms employed. The extreme type of this fault can be seen in the popular sentimental song melody that pivots around the fifth degree of a major or minor key and so often remains there while the accompanying parts lead to a close upon the tonic triad, *pp*.

Not the least among the problems which are brought up by this principle of the false repetition is this question: When is a tone a repeated one and when is it not? The present tendency toward the acceptance of the duodecuple scale leaves us, theoretically, with only twelve tones per octave, obviously a serious come-down from the pitch resources during the period 1700–1900, when there were certainly not less than forty or fifty per octave. (The reader who does not understand the phenomenon described by Rameau as *double emploi* may need to be reassured that it is not alleged here that the piano of Beethoven and Brahms had forty or more tones per octave, but that each of the twelve tones in each octave served for from four to eight other tones, being a little off-tune for the other tones it is true, but not so far off but that the ear could twist it to fit the structural pattern of the prevailing tonality.) Thus, one may question whether the E flat in the second measure of "Portals" should be written so or written D sharp. If one thinks of it as D sharp, an undesirable repetition is felt when, at the end of the fourth measure, B natural-D sharp occurs. The passage appears correctly written, therefore, and the E flat, if it has any conventional implications, should be regarded as harmonically associated with the G and C before it rather than with the B and F sharp after it.

Whether the listener, hearing this but not seeing the score or thinking about the problem, will understand an E flat or a D sharp depends, of course, upon the manner of the rendition. If a good low E flat is taken and, the second progression after, a good high F sharp, there will be less chance that the falseness with the fourth measure will be felt. The danger here is extreme, for though there have been nine progressions before the repetition of the B natural, the repetition is a double one: E flat - B natural against B natural - D sharp. On a piano, allegro, the falseness might be quite striking; but on the orchestra it is not, or need not be. Furthermore, the slow tempo serves to dissonate, where a fast one would tend to consonate, the situation.

The validity of the principle under discussion also depends upon the generality of the sensitiveness to repetition. If Ruggles had produced a large body of work exemplifying, elaborating, and cultivating (I almost said teaching) this, more could be said for it. It is true that a number of independent workers have developed this sensitiveness and formulated principles of like sort. There can be no doubt, however, that it demands an increase in the number of degrees in the octave, either tempered or "natural" (not enough is known of the relation between acoustics and psychology and musical practice for it to be said what "natural" is). For the present, Ruggles' tacit adoption of a 21-tone scale (seven "white" tones with a sharp and a flat for each) is in keeping with the best practice in present-day notation and certainly has good sense back of it, though one often wonders why he uses accidentals as he does. Often as not, ease in reading seems to be the guide, convenient for the player, but devastating to the student.

Summing up this brief consideration of an important problem, there is no doubt that Ruggles' principle makes for a clean line. In its avoidance of the cliché it runs into the danger of becoming itself a cliché. So far, as a perusal of "Portals" quickly shows (cf. Violin II, measures 14–15), he has not applied his principle too strictly. It may, however, be accepted as useful and, if not applied with too great rigor, can be modified by devices such as "pivoting" and "anchoring." But it is undoubtedly more an instrumental than a vocal principle. As such it may be important in freeing composition from the last vestiges of vocal influence—a process in operation for several centuries. (No implication of good or evil must be understood!) Taken broadly, the reiterated and repeated tone would, in Ruggles' music, infuse

[27

a rhetorical, a theatrical, a lax quality that would be most undesirable. One awaits with considerable interest the American performance of the "Sun-Treader" for an indication of the highest development of this principle of avoidance.

Other outstanding characteristics of the melodic line are: the rather broad upward and downward curves of the more declamatory passages and the very twisting, shorter-sectioned *pianissimo* passages; the rather general avoidance of the dance or sectional phraseology; and the reliance upon a prose rather than upon a verse construction. There is practically no metrical accent, the complex sequence of signatures being used more for rhythmic or phrase accentuation. The continuity of the line is more clearly felt in the compositions for instruments of the same kind (as, e.g., in "Angels," "Lilacs," and "Portals") than in those for diverse instruments. Clearly, the necessity of avoiding repeated tones, especially until such a large gap has occurred, makes the composition of a melody very difficult. Indeed, it is a question whether Ruggles is not curbing his Pegasus unduly and hence restricting his output by an increasing devotion to his principle. No one can say. Of all the people in the world who "know what is best for a composer to do," we must give precedence to the composer himself!

The chordal material is very varied. Having constructed a fine chord progression, Ruggles is prone to add an extra line or so. But the increase in contrapuntal feeling evinced by the later works will tend to restrict this harmonic exuberance. The harmonic variety, added to the extreme floridity of the melodic and contrapuntal fabric, gives one a feeling of having heard a great deal in a very short time. None of the works are long. "Portals," the most substantial up to the

"Sun-Treader," lasts not more than four and a half minutes. This compactness is a great virtue in modern music. How often, at concerts of modern music, listening to seemingly endless symphonies, quartets, trios, reminiscent of Dvořák and Rubinstein and Strauss, has one felt as if looking through the wrong end of a telescope and seeing very little!

The form is mainly rhapsodic. Being so short and not built upon the development-of-a-theme idea, even the minimum of recapitulation indulged in could probably be dispensed with in most of the pieces. Two-part form, in which the second part is a very abbreviated version of the first, is the general rule except in the "Sun-Treader," whose greater length (50 pages) shows a number of parts (perhaps half a dozen or so) and in "Portals" where the two parts are of equal length, resembling each other only in initial material, with a short introduction to the first and a short coda (one of the most exquisite pages in all modern music!) to the second.

To make now a stretto of the somewhat casually assembled strands of this sketch, it may be well to propose that, theoretically at least, any composition should represent an approximate balance of the various considerations involved. Largest among these is the perennial conflict between the technical and the critical—the facts of the medium and the values they embody. Obviously, Ruggles' strength is in his critical determinations. There he is positive, unwavering. Technically, his position is weak. He is in this weak position because, as has been already pointed out, he was born at a time when the current technique of music was being questioned—and under the questioning it disintegrated. He is one of those who did the questioning, but not by any means the only one. In this realm one man cannot do much. A technique is a communal, a manifold thing. If the materials of the art of music are ever assembled into a new style comparable to that of the great styles of the past—of Bach, of Beethoven, of Palestrina—Ruggles will be among the men who will have contributed to its making. It was Izaak, Zarlino, Gabrieli, Monteverdi, Gesualdo, Frescobaldi, Schütz, Froberger, Buxtehude, and hundreds of others that made the work of Bach possible. It is only the technique of textbook writing with its jejune hero-worship that makes anyone think Bach did it all himself. All hail to the great man. But would not he, and with justice, too, be the very first to acknowledge what he owed to his known and unknown predecessors? We cannot say that the man makes the times or the times make the man. It is nip and tuck between them. Perhaps Bach did contribute by his sheer personal power more than fifty per cent of the value of his work. But where is the unit of measure—or even the principle of measurement? We simply have no such thing. Yet we have to act as if there were a ratio of praise and blame. Fifty-fifty, I say. Maybe a little more here, a little less there. But for every attribute of greatness, for every deficiency in a man there can be produced a corresponding one in his materials, those materials that have been given a certain constitution and character by the sum-total of the work of his predecessors, sung and unsung. Ruggles' technical deficiencies, then, are not of his own making. We all suffer from the instability, the eclecticism, the hashed-up state of our musical art as it came to us from our musical fathers. There is one thing that can be said of him that can be said of very few indeed: His work is reminiscent of no other man, school, or style.

Small as the body of it is, it stands quite distinct and *sui generis*. No tricks or novelties either!

The technique as a whole shows a curious ratio between organization and fantasy. Assuming, as we may, again theoretically, that a work of art should present an approximate balance (approaching, though it does not necessarily reach, a meticulous balance) between the two—organism and fantasy —it would appear that in Ruggles' work there is a vast preponderance of fantasy. Of all the many factors in the technique of music (and there are dozens of them of the "size" or importance of the one he has organized) only the repeated-tone is organized. And even there, in the published works, the principle evolved is often broken! One feels it was almost in despair of the difficulty of the task set. But though one feels the works to be imperfect, though one knows that, given half an excuse, Ruggles would rip them to pieces and rewrite almost every measure, still, in the hearing, especially of "Angels," "Lilacs," and "Portals," one knows that one has heard a complete work of art, the effect and the memory of which lies over and above the recognized and admitted imperfections. In spite of the reams of theoretical explanations, bizarre and, from a scholarly point of view, preposterous, that Ruggles is accustomed to regale his listeners with, here is pure intuition. The pool is muddied, the banks are cluttered up, and the surface is rippled; but one knows after one leaves it that one has had an unforgettable intimation of the clear, unsullied crystal. "What are those of the known but to ascend and enter the Unknown?" What, indeed?

As to Ruggles' critique as a whole, here again is unbalance, where a theoretical balance should be. It must be remembered, in this respect, that musical criticism is given, primarily, in music itself, just as is musical technique. Musical value, and the expression and communication of it, is primarily the function of the composer—only secondarily should we look for its exposition in language. Hence every composition embodies, among other things, a critique of the art of its day, a revision of its criteria, a reappraisal of its values. Ruggles has not informed himself historico-critically of the past, nor has he bothered much with the question of the social usefulness of his aims or his deeds. But here again we come face to face with the same enigma (or else it is not an enigma, but the most obvious sort of experience) —*the beauty is there*, or *is near*. What is lacked in balance is there in conviction—sheer arrogant assertion—of value. You cannot put your finger on it. You cannot point out any melody, passage, or detail that even represents it or can be characterized as such. But you know, just as surely, that in hearing the work you have been in touch with, or had intimations of, the sublime. The known enters the unknown (or vice versa). The critic who attempts in language to be logical can go only so far. He can point out that the means-by-which have certain virtues and faults, but it is very hard, when there is so little attempt at organization, to relate these to the experience which has so evanescent yet so real a temporal relation with them.

Perhaps this is in part due to the peculiarity of the work. Perhaps, too, the nearness in time and space, and the bias, personal, nationalist, or racial, makes matters still more difficult. Of course, a complete criticism (something this sketch cannot pretend to be) should have both its scientific-critical, or logical, section and its impressionistic, or rhapsodic, one. But in treating of Carl Ruggles, it is impossible to do justice to the former without writing a history of music and a manual of modern composition, not to mention a ponderous treatise upon musicological method. And to do justice to the latter is so easy! "The best that has come from America—as distinctive as Poe and Whitman—almost to be valued for what it tries to do rather than for what it actually achieves—promising great things for the future of American music—but tragic in its plucky but hopeless attempt to grow in such musically arid ground, such musically rare atmosphere as that of the great New Rome's."

What a great unwieldy corpus this American music is—great talent, great resources, great opportunities; but still a giant without head or feet—no folk-art for us to stand on, no head to direct us. Crutches and guidebooks we borrow uncritically from Europe and think we are dancing finely! And it is in connection with such a monstrosity that we wish to evaluate this work so delicate, so elusive, so recherché! What if it is unbalanced both technically and critically? How could it be otherwise? Shades of John Sebastian! it should be just what it is. To set straight such a lop-sided giant one has to be just as lop-sided, but in an opposite direction. And that is what Carl Ruggles is. Do the Europeans look to our serious composers to be what Europe thinks is the spirit of America? Let them look elsewhere than to Ruggles; he is almost the exact opposite of everything that is supposed to be typically American. Thank heaven! And he is not alone—there are a few others. If there are not, and if they are not given some kind of support, American music will never be anything but a pale reflection of the European art, even as Rome's art was of the art of the Hellenes! There is a certain European jury that for two years has persistently disregarded the recommendation of "Portals." They seem to prefer American works that show "the jazz influence." How would the French feel if at an international festival their art were held representable only by works showing the influence of eighteenth-century chansons? How would the Germans feel if three or four Strauss waltzes (or imitations of them) were chosen to represent theirs? Jazz is as insignificant a development of American music as either of those charming but particularly small and curious genres. Serious American music has nothing more in common with it than has serious European. And incidentally let it be said by one who *does* appreciate good jazz that there has not come to my notice one single treatment of jazz in so-called "art-music" that did not lower the value of the work as art and fail utterly to be one-tenth as good music, arty or otherwise, as the half-asleep improvisation of any good Negro dance-hall band. "Educated" jazz is a popularization of European art-music—Brahms and Wagner, especially, liberally seasoned with Debussy. For European or American musicians with serious minds to trifle with this mere compost of their art is not only fatal to the single work but indicates better than anything else the bankruptcy of the whole romantic style. *"Il faut cultiver nos jardins!"* Yes—but eat the fruit, not the fertilizer.

Ruggles' refusal to be popular in any form is as refreshing as his abjuration of jazz. Of course, this restricts his audience and leaves him an artist for artists. He would be greater, with a greater appeal—that goes without saying. And it can be said of anyone, even Bach. There is not much sense in it. We should be more thankful for what people are and less worried about what they are not. "Holy mackerel!" I hear Carl say, "I am a social force am I? Well—you have a great head and are probably right." So he will try arguing with the town postmaster that the artist is a misunderstood martyr for social progress. The next night he will take on the local ne'er-do-well, maintaining, in a heated debate, the non-socialness of art. Having tried both sides he will forget all about both and get back to composition again, using select pieces of wrapping paper of varying colors and sizes, ruling his own staff-lines about one inch apart so that the notes are grand and fat, made often as not with colored crayon. And the "Sun-Treader" presently will stand out as a landmark. Between 1750 and 1931 there will be a valley, filled with a blue haze through which some almost indistinguishable forms can still be seen, though dimly, to be possibilities not realized in the past that may be realized in the future.

Adolph Weiss and Colin McPhee

This is an attempt not to evaluate the works of either Weiss or McPhee, or even to give my impressions of their music as such, but to analyze their works in a purely objective way.

These left-wing composers began (as have many of their modernist confreres) by following the beaten path in their early works, refuting a belief, popular among conservatives, that "modernists" either have abjured the conventional idiom through inability to master it or are using modernist tactics to impress the public. I quote first from some early songs of Weiss—that is, early in his creative life, which began rather late. Here are a few measures toward the close of his "Nachtlied" (1915):

The following are impressionistic. This one, from "The Railway Train," was written in 1925:

An earlier bit, from "A Cemetery," was written the previous year (1924):

Unfortunately McPhee's earlier works are inaccessible to me at present, but, according to his own account, he also fell quite naturally into the accepted idiom, his teachers wondering at his gift for improvising. His "Morte d'Arthur," which he played in Baltimore (1920) with the Baltimore Symphony Orchestra, was a decided success, from which we infer that it in no way challenged the audience in their comfortable rut of musical thinking.

The conclusion then would be that both of these composers developing along conservative lines would have achieved a plausible success; yet we find Weiss going on a pilgrimage to Vienna to study with the arch-heretic, Schoenberg, and McPhee shocking his hearers with his "Piano Concerto" in Toronto (1924).

Weiss now employs (although by no means exclusively) a 12-tone row technique. A series of twelve different tones, in any of their thousands of possible arrangements, is but the starting-point of a composition—what a stone is to a building. It is as far from determining the style of a work as is the major scale, so that we find Weiss employing it to express many moods. In his sonata for flute and viola we find the following row at the beginning:

Later this is transformed into a spiritedly rhythmic theme:

The first half of this theme is the inversion of the tone row, while the second half is the row inverted and backwards. For melodic reasons the register of individual notes is occasionally changed and single notes or groups of notes are repeated. All of this is illustrated in the example quoted and suggests endless possibilities. Sometimes a section of the row is repeated many times, with an ostinato effect, against which we may have the entire row in another voice in any contrapuntal or rhythmic variation. Only a study of the score (published by *New Music*) can convey an idea of the polyphonic possibilities of this variety of technic.

Further examples of Weiss's 12-tone row procedure are herewith quoted from his own analysis of No. 3 of his six piano preludes (published in *New Music*):

No. VI is a twelve-tone row built up horizontally by third-steps, and which continues its melodic line by its own crab- and inverted forms. The figuration of the right hand always brings that part of the twelve-tone row not used in the left hand (the melodic line).

Nos. XI and XII consist of twelve-tone rows in four forms, the first the natural form, the second the inverted form, the third the crab-form of the natural form, the fourth the crab-form of the inverted form. These various forms are combined simultaneously throughout, horizontally and vertically. No. XII is in three-part form, of which the second part is a crab-form of the first part and the third a crab-form of the second part. The tonal sequences are always strict, though rhythmically free.

Instead of using a row of twelve tones (sometimes fewer) as a starting-point, Weiss sometimes takes one or two intervals and with these builds up an entire work. His *Kammersymphonie* is based on the augmented fourth and minor seventh; his "American Life" on the augmented fourth alone, or its equivalent, the diminished fifth. I quote the following themes from the latter work, all of which show this characteristic interval:

Notice that it is the first and last notes of each group of three notes which give us the augmented fourth.

Here the augmented fourths are mostly vertical instead of horizontal; that is, in the first chord, G sharp down to D, etc.

I have pointed out a few of the peculiarities of this special kind of technique, the stressing of which is apt to give a wrong impression of Weiss's work. I have in mind a theme beginning with the interval vibration-ratios 4:5, 5:6, then 9:8. We will admit that this is hardly an adequate description of the finale of Beethoven's *Fifth Symphony!*

Let me, then, brush the academic dust away long enough to hint that "American Life" may be more than sublimated, augmented fourth. I feel that it reflects our sentimentality, our nervous energy, and something of our morbid love of the sensational, just as I sense something of the ironical to be present in the "Kammersymphonie."

Before analyzing McPhee's works I think it well to give his own statement regarding his recent creative work:

The "Concerto" [for piano and wind octette] represents the time when I was chiefly interested in economy of means and formalism. "Mechanical Principles" shows my change to more elaborate material, form, rhythm, the use of polytonality, etc. From that work on I have been trying to express through music an emotion resulting from contact with daily life—its noise, rhythm, energy, and mechanical daring. Do not think I mean program music. I have no more definite, concrete idea in mind than the construction of logical music whose rhythms derive from mechanics, whose tonal structure, while orderly and complete, is as complex as the structure of a large bridge. My output has been small for the past few years, as I have found difficulty in finding myself and have mistrusted my natural facility.

I purposely quote this last statement of McPhee's, showing as it does the tendency of most creative artists to doubt the validity of their inspiration. It reminds one of the perplexed cenobite at the beginning of *Thaïs*, wondering if his dream emanates from God or the devil. A certain amount of doubt is healthy, but the lot of the perpetual doubter (in this sense) is not to be envied. Luckily McPhee's period of excessive doubt seems to be at an end.

I will not show proofs of his "economy of means" by quoting passages from his piano octette, but will rather call attention to some of his rhythmic devices. Here is a passage from the Finale (piano part) showing groups of three in a rhythm of four in the left hand, and in the right a rhythmical shift (*Verschiebung*) of the four sixteenth-notes from the fourth beat to the third beat and back again to the fourth:

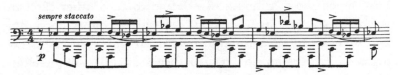

Here is another shift in the right hand against groups of five in the left, showing also the logical consummation of the phrase:

I quote still another treatment of the same material, shifted

rhythm against the rhythm of three eighth-notes in the orchestra (beginning with the third measure).

I have heard "Mechanical Principles" but do not have the score to quote from. I felt a different and more subtle texture there than in the "Concerto," an evident foreshadowing of the change of style which McPhee now seems to be undergoing.

I have looked over McPhee's two piano pieces appearing in *New Music* ("Kinesis" and "Invention") and feel it rather hard to quote from them. Each seems to have been conceived as a unit (though probably it was not!), so that the phrases have much more meaning in relation to each other than in themselves. This, far from being derogatory, implies breadth, and it seems to me a leaning toward the larger forms of expression rather than a lyricism per se, while not precluding it.

His "Sea Chanty Suite," the only other work which I have examined, is a highly effective setting of six Scottish airs for baritone solo, men's chorus, two pianos, and six kettledrums.

Edgar Varèse *

Edgar Varèse was born in France, but has become an American citizen. For many years he lived in New York, and through his vehicle, the International Composers' Guild, he was the first to introduce modern music to America with any degree of consistency. Thus he has been an influence in the development of new musical ideas in America; and his fostering of many American composers and his presentation of their works were the only things which encouraged them in maintaining a modernism of style which prevented them from being performed elsewhere for a long time. Many of these are now recognized as of importance.

Varèse's own music has nothing in particular to do with America otherwise. It was originated in Europe under the influence of his teacher, Busoni, and was also affected by the Italian "futurist" school of percussionists. However, his best work, "Arcane," was written in America, and his longest work is called "Amérique," indicating very well just what the work is—a Frenchman's concept of America! His music is acrid and telling, with a magnificent hardness of line which used to irritate our naïve listeners greatly, as did also his investigations in the field of emphasis on percussion sounds.

In making his music Varèse breaks no rules of ordinary harmony; they do not come into consideration at all, as they do not pertain to that different art which is his aim. This does not mean, however, that he follows no rules. To attain

*Varèse now spells Edgar with a final "d."

his ends, he is forced into certain limitations which one might call rules of his own making, as will be seen.

In order to make technical references, it is necessary here to expand the meaning of certain musical terms. Let us assume that the word melody refers to any succession of single tones, without reference to whether or not it is immediately pleasing, follows certain curves, or is contained within a key. The word harmony will refer to any group of tones played simultaneously. And any succession of accents, note-values, or rates of speed will be considered as rhythm.

One key to a comprehension of Varèse's music is the fact that he is more interested in finding a note that will sound a certain way in a certain instrument and will "sound" in the orchestral fabric than he is in just what position the note occupies in the harmony; except, of course, in so far as its harmonic position will pertain to its "coming out" in the scoring.

One must consider that besides the harmony of notes, which with Varèse is somewhat secondary, there is at any given time also a harmony of tone-qualities, each of which is calculated to sound out through the orchestra. For example Varèse will use a certain chord. Superimposed upon this chord, and more important than the harmony itself to Varèse, is the harmony resultant from the tone qualities of the instruments owing to their particular sound in the register in which he scores each; so that, while the chord might be found in many a modern composer's work, it assumes a character found only in Varèse when we see it in his particular scoring.

I have frequently noticed that when Varèse examines a new score, he is more interested in the orchestration than in the musical content, although no amount of brilliant scoring will interest him in a work in old-fashioned style.

Just as harmonic combinations of sound qualities are emphasized above harmony itself by Varèse, one finds that dynamic nuances on the same note, or repeated tones, often take the place of melody. He very frequently does away with melody entirely by having only repeated tones for certain passages. Removing from the listener's ear that which it is accustomed to follow most closely, sometimes almost to the exclusion of everything else, naturally induces a keener awareness of other musical elements such as rhythm and dynamics. Varèse, however, is always careful to supply the ear with subtleties of dynamic change which take the place of melody in certain passages. Owing to his reliance on specific tone-qualities and dynamics for the very essence of his music, there are dynamic markings and directions as to quality applying to nearly every note in Varèse's scores. Sometimes a single note will have a number of signs, as for instance a certain note in the trumpet part of "Octandre" which is marked *sf, diminuendo, p, crescendo, sfff.* I have heard Varèse express great contempt for composers who do not use many expression marks. "They do not know how they wish their music to sound," he says.

Sometimes Varèse cuts out melody to call attention to the rhythm rather than dynamics. The opening of the second movement of "Octandre" is a long flute solo, of a type which would ordinarily contain a long melodic curve. Varèse uses only repeated tones, with two or three grace notes to relieve the monotony of pitch. This introduction is in the form of five rhythmical phrases, all different, and separated by longer notes.

In "Hyperprism," page ten, we find a good example of the discontinuance of the melody (partly by repeated tones and partly, as in the flute and trumpets, by continued repetition of a figure) for the purpose of calling attention to the cross-rhythm between the parts. There is a combination of two, three, and four against each other, and in the center of the last measure a quarter-note triplet of particular interest, since it begins and ends on a weak beat, running through the strong beat; the second note, being accented, almost but not quite coincides with the third beat of the measure in an extremely unusual manner. Varèse evidently realized that these rhythmical subtleties would be lost on the listener, were his attention to be diverted by melodic interest or harmonic change.

It is perhaps this desire to focus the interest on harmonies of sound-quality alone—without the distraction of harmonies of pitch—or on chords of rhythms, that has led Varèse to develop his emphasis on the percussion instruments. He probably uses more such instruments, proportionately, than any other composer. For example in "Hyperprism" there are seventeen percussion as against nine melodic instruments. Sometimes he uses percussion passages alone, but more often the percussion is in connection with some of the other instruments. His "Ionization" is for battery alone.

In "Hyperprism," page eight, there is a good illustration of a simple chord combination of tone-qualities. First a chord composed of the qualities of Indian drum, bass drum, tambourine, and cymbal against each other moves to a chord of snare drum, crash-cymbal, tam-tam, and slap-stick, which in turn progresses back to the first combination—a sort of four-part harmony. On page sixteen, measure two, there is an example of rhythmic harmony, as each instrument has an independent rhythm.

An analysis of the rhythms throughout "Hyperprism" reveals a great variety of rhythmic figures. On the first page alone there are thirty-two different rhythmical manners of filling a measure. Through the whole work there are surprisingly few rhythmical duplications. It has been said by those who perceive a minimum of tonal, melodic, and harmonic changes in his music that Varèse lacks invention; yet undoubtedly for the development of so many different figures of rhythm one must concede as great inventive fertility as is usually recognized in the field of pitch.

Varèse does not ignore melody and harmony, but merely does away with them on occasion. He limits himself almost exclusively to harmonies containing strong dissonances, i.e., minor seconds or ninths, and major sevenths. One may therefore say that he has developed for himself a rule that such dissonant intervals are requisite for the harmonic fabric he desires. To introduce a consonant harmony would remove the sense of implacable, resilient hardness, and create a weak link in the chain; the let-down would be so great that the whole composition might fall to pieces. Varèse's chords are obviously not haphazard, but belong to a special category in which he is careful to have certain general proportions of different sorts of intervals.

Melody, when Varèse uses it, is often characterized by wide skips, broken sometimes by chromatic passages, as, for example, in "Hyperprism," flute part, page five. Sometimes the wide skips are broken by repeated tones, as in the voice part of "La Croix du Sud," page three, from "Offrandes."

One rhythmical innovation used by Varèse is his metrical marking of 3/4 and a half, 1/4 and a half, 4/4 and a half, and so forth. The extra one-half represents in each case an added half-beat, or eighth-note, at the end of the measure. Some musicians claim that 1/4 and a half time is really the same as 3/8 time, since it contains the same number of eighth-notes in a measure. There is, however, a great distinction in the rhythmical feeling between these two signatures, as 3/8 is smooth-flowing, and is conducted in three movements of the baton, while 1/4 and a half is irregular, and is led by one longer followed by one shorter stroke of the conductor's stick.

There is a dramatic and incisive element about Varèse's music which causes it to stand out on a program, and to "kill" any work standing next to it by brute force. This does not mean that the music is better or worse; but it is unquestionably telling. And if stirring auditors to an almost unendurable irritation be taken into account, then the music can be said to be highly emotional. While he lacks melodic invention and harmonic succession, Varèse is in other respects unique, and deserves the highest place among European composers who have become American.

Aaron Copland

Someone has said that Aaron Copland's musical ideas are like pennies shrewdly invested rather than pearls advantageously set. This is not a fair statement, since it might imply that his works are mere skillful fabrications, which is far from the case. It would be more accurate to say that his architectural sense is in advance of his sense of style, which is still impure. For though it is true that his work as a whole is less often remarkable for distinction of material than for the power of construction and development displayed in presenting it, yet there are pearls, too, though these are not always in their perfect settings. In all questions of balancing tonalities, of negotiating transitions, of building up climaxes, and preparing cadences, Copland generally shows a flawless ear and sense of proportion. Moreover, his faculty for discovering unexpected resources in his material, for presenting it under all sorts of different aspects, always alive and essentially musical, shows great imaginative force, amply compensating his lack of richness or abundance in initial ideas.

What is still lacking, on occasion, is a kind of integrity of sensibility, something to give more than a picturesque, or, in certain cases, a merely formal unity to his work. This lack is chiefly apparent in his more ambitiously personal works, such as the early "Symphony for Organ and Orchestra," and in his latest composition, a "Symphonic Ode." As a positive limitation it is perhaps least apparent in the "Trio," one of his ablest performances, foreshadowing in

[49

style certain characteristics of the "Ode," but achieving greater unity in this respect than the latter. This is doubtless partly accounted for by the smaller scale on which the "Trio"* was planned, but it is due also to a certain picturesqueness in its unity, almost as of a convincing character sketch. Eloquent and moving as certain passages are (especially the close), it impresses one rather as a prosperous excursion into a somewhat limited and special field, than as the full expression of a personality.

The same thing might be said of the "Concerto" for piano and orchestra (1926), despite its great brilliance. If there was anything to be done on a symphonic plan, with the material and idiom of jazz, it is certain that in this "Concerto" Copland has triumphantly succeeded in doing it. The finale is essentially jazz, but in no sense is it dance music—which is less of a paradox than it might seem, since the whole problem was to find the appropriate and independent form for that material, to give it autonomy. This is precisely what Copland has done.

There is, however, one error in the way he builds up the climax of the first movement. After a series of four effectively dovetailed entrances of a long, expressive phrase for the strings, the four strands of melody become so matted that the ear can scarcely disentangle them. Supporting this is a heavy harmonic foundation, whose reiterated and uniform motion, sufficient to attract the ear as a kind of refuge from the intricacies of the upper structure, is nevertheless too heavy and mechanical to add much life to the movement of the whole. Were the bass's movements less perceptible,

---

* "Vitebsk," study on a Jewish melody, for piano, violin, and 'cello, written about 1929.

50]

one would forget them, and strain to follow the complicated pattern unfolding itself above. Were they, on the other hand, freer and more alive, it might perhaps add further intricacies to what is intricate enough already, but at least it would be homogeneous with the rest: the ear might then have nowhere to go, but this would be preferable to sitting dully in a cellar.

Apart from this miscalculation (which might well be less apparent at a good performance than one perceives from knowing the score, or from having heard it badly played), the "Concerto" can hardly be found fault with. The zest which he manages to instill into certain rather jaded jazz *motifs,* the skilful disposition of the material, the humor and perfect timing of contrasts (not to mention the tense excitement of the close, with its alternating rhythmic bounds and sudden, quivering halts, as though immobilized by its very excess of energy) save this work from being in any sense a *pastiche,* though one is aware of potentialities in Copland, not realized here, of achieving a more fruitfully personal style.

More ambitious, but in a way less successful than the "Concerto," less of an accomplished *tour de force,* but richer in promises, is the "Symphonic Ode." In all preceding works, his essential personality has seemed fragmentary, not wholly liberated. I do not find it wholly liberated even in the "Ode," but the direction in which his style is tending is much clearer and more decisively individual than it has ever appeared before. The whole first section—the marshaling of those ponderous blocks at the beginning, the vast inertia with which they shift and settle, reluctant to get under way, yet acquiring momentum inevitably, until they reach the point where they must break up and scatter into the feathery brightness of the Allegro—in the breadth and gravity of this music one feels that Copland has at last brought to light an essence which is entirely his own.

There are one or two harmonic idiosyncrasies in this work, such as his constant use of an interval or chord of two widely spaced notes (a "tenth," to be exact), for which he has an untiring preference. It cannot be denied that certain of the uses he puts it to make one see something in this interval, in its color-value, that one never saw before. But at other times there seems to be no reason at all for his using it, except perhaps to be consistent, though the recurrence of what is hardly more than a mannerism is surely not what gives a style consistency. Again, in a transitional passage leading up to the Più mosso ancora (which in turn bridges over to the Allegro), there is some unnecessarily disagreeable dissonance arising from the way the bass is written. While two horns are slowly covering a wide upward stretch in parallel straight lines, and the violins, an octave higher, embroider on these two lines, pointing and enhancing their upward movement, the bass, having only a small distance downward to cover in the same period, and being consequently in no hurry, dawdles and fumbles along, getting in everyone's way. One wishes Copland had found more profitable things for it to do with its spare time.

The first of these peculiarities of style—the repeated use of the same chord—can perhaps be attributed to a certain poverty of harmonic resource which is noticeable in a good deal of his work, and is evinced also by his frequent use of *ostinati*. (It is possibly the basis of what Paul Rosenfeld refers to as Copland's "leanness.") The second peculiarity of style is of much smaller consequence. One cannot, on the strength of this one short passage, call Copland's way of writing careless, for there is, in the same work alone, far too much evidence to the contrary; for example, at the Poco più mosso not far from the beginning, where, over the calm reverberations of a figure deep in the bass (assigned to piano and harp), a muted trumpet, a clarinet, a flute, and an oboe call and answer each other with different fragments of the theme—all in dark and mysteriously spacious tranquillity. There is a shift of key very near the beginning of this passage, so delicate as to be almost imperceptible in its passing, yet of itself enough to show that Copland is anything but insensible to the most subtle inflections of musical language.

So far as his melodic style goes, in certain works previous to the Ode one had glimpses of it (in the Prelude of "Music for the Theatre" and in the "Lento Molto" for string quartet), but hardly more. The theme of the Ode, and its first developments, show a marked advance in substantiality and strength of line over anything written before. While the long melody that runs through the first movement of the Concerto seems to arise out of an "atmosphere" or ambient mood of sultry lyricism, and the theme of the finale of the "Symphony for Organ and Orchestra" seems groping in its contours, that of the Ode is entirely self-sufficient and definitive. One may, perhaps, find his presentation of it too obviously declamatory (full brasses flanked by heavy accents in the bass and high treble), but this does not prevent it from speaking for itself, as a line of powerful impulse and free flight.

He is again, melodically, at his best in the beginning of the slow middle section, where the initial phrase of the same theme, from having been at first stretched out to cover a wide span, is here reduced to its smallest compass (using the same notes). This procedure, together with the really genial harmonies that accompany it, give a reserved and recollected character to these measures, perhaps the finest in his entire work. But here again he allows us only a glimpse of what might be; for the style of this section as a whole is mixed and fragmentary. We are given the beginning of a line, of great sobriety and distinction, but in what follows one feels that Copland has become involved in "figures" and inventions. Attractive as these figures are, and ingenious as developments of the initial idea, they are somehow on a less serious, a more "atmospheric" and mood-engendered, plane than that on which he started. Even where he gives the theme in slow syncopation to the English horn—charmingly rounding off each phrase, once by an unexpected drop at the penultimate, the next time by a corresponding rise, and a floating, weaving, suspended repetition of the last two notes —though by all odds a "good moment," even this is not really in keeping with the beginning; nor is the in itself beautifully written part later on, where the second period of the original theme, played by the violas, rises like a fragrant exhalation out of a rich fabric of lower voices; nor that where the violins subsequently take up the same phrase, on an almost too caressing change of key.

It is not through any lack of talent that he goes astray here. Considered apart from their context, these passages are all pleasing enough. It is rather, as I remarked at the beginning of this study, a unifying integrity of style which is lacking.

The last part of the Ode, or rather the recapitulation and

expansion of the Allegro, may seem musically empty. The occasion, however, did not call for new material of importance. Its length will seem excessive only if one forgets the scale on which the piece started. Having opened in such a roundly declamatory, almost grandiloquent, manner, it was necessary to work up to that pitch again, and, at the close, to surpass it. The preparation of the final tonality, the last measures, where eight horns *fortissimo* stride upward till they reach a dizzy peak—all this is realized in a masterly manner. Nor is there any actual weakening or falling off in the rather barren slopes which precede this climax and build it up. One only regrets, perhaps, that he should have placed his peak at such a sensational height that all vegetation ceases long before we reach it. In other words, it is possible that the work as a whole would have gained in purity and in concision of style through being reduced in scale.

In conclusion it must be added that such detailed criticism as I have attempted on the work of a man of only thirty-two, the bulk and average merit of whose performance to date are so remarkable, should not be taken too seriously. The limitations one is conscious of are by no means necessarily inherent; nor can they, as I have said, be ascribed to want of talent, for of this he has already shown sufficient abundance to place him in the front rank of contemporary musicians.

[Since the foregoing article was written, Aaron Copland has produced a number of new works, and has materially broadened his tendencies in composition. For one thing, he no longer relies on jazz themes to animate his auditors. In his "Variations for Piano," which is perhaps his most important recent work, he takes a very quiet thematic germ, consisting for the most part of a skip of the interval of a major third, and, through variation, forms from this simple material a well-knit work of broad outline, which contains both sharply incisive dissonant bite and lyric persuasiveness.—H. C.]

CHAPTER VI: BY NICOLAS SLONIMSKY

Henry Cowell

It is rare to find a crusader in a big cause whose intellect is as strong as his battle-ax. Not all crusaders are more interested in their cause than in themselves. Few are creators of original work in a field of art. Henry Cowell is the exceptional type who possesses all of these qualities. In Pushkin's fantastic tale of Mozart and Salieri, there are these amazing lines:

> And I dissected music as a corpse,
> By algebra I tested harmony of sounds, ...

This scientific procedure Henry Cowell unashamedly resumes. If there is one rule in his creative work, it consists in taking nothing for granted. Harmony, rhythm, tonecolor—Henry Cowell submits them to a test as if they were mere human beliefs, not divine laws.

Henry Cowell's life-story includes many adventurous chapters—born in California, of intellectual parents, he lived in the freedom of the hospitable country, without benefit of an estate or even as much property as would insure safe transition from infancy into adulthood. Having had no compulsory education, he conjectured and speculated by himself, unaided and unhindered. Musical sounds around him fascinated him as suitable material for synthetical experiments. When he first got hold of a decrepit upright piano, he discovered new possibilities on it. Considerably later, when he revealed to astonished audiences gathered in New York, San Francisco, London, Berlin, Paris, Warsaw, and Moscow

[57

what could be done with the grand piano, he was merely developing his first-hand knowledge derived from these earlier experiences. At some intervening date he thought up a convenient terminology. He was scientific as well as pictorial when he named a group of keys struck with the forearm a "tone-cluster"; a compound fairly threatening to break into the sacrosanct pages of Grove's *Dictionary of Music,* for the lack of another descriptive name and from the necessity of designating a musical phenomenon which, however unpalatable to purists, is forcing itself irrepressibly into musical existence. Cowell had many years of conventional study, but only after he had already created, developed, and scientifically systematized an individual style of his own. When the first shock resulting from the exterior appearance of his piano-playing passed, intelligent people found that there is sound harmonic sense in the use of complete blocks of sounds, diatonically or chromatically arranged, treated as indivisible units. Our musical generation saw the use of triads in parallel construction, as if they were unisons or octaves; and, in polytonal writing, still bulkier entities were liberally handled. Apart from the question of using one's antebrachia for the production of "tone-clusters," there is nothing unacceptable in the idea to the seasoned musician; on the other hand, it is a logical development of modern harmonic resources.

Thus, from innocent experimenting with the acoustical possibilities latent in an ordinary piano, Cowell came to conclusions of harmonic order. Experimenting with the soundboard of the grand piano led him to discoveries in the field of tone-color. Everyone who has heard his weird glissandos, interpretive of the ghost of his Irish ancestors, "The Banshee," rendered directly on the piano strings, will admit that as a new orchestral color it is an undeniable acquisition. Pizzicato on the piano strings, as well as the entire gamut of percussion, conjured up from the pianistic entrails, make the piano a richer instrument without impinging on its historical dignity. As an orchestral instrument, Cowell's string and percussion piano (that is, the ordinary piano enriched by extraordinary applications) ought to be used whenever a masculine harp tone is required, and for new battery sounds not obtainable on drums or cymbals.

Henry Cowell, as a composer, made an early start. Before he was twenty, in the midst of distracting activities in rural and pastoral life around the paternal shack in which he was born and which is still his only sedentary home-sweet-home, he had composed music of all descriptions, including a symphony and an opera. At the same vigesimal calendas he delved for the first time into the problems of notation. This latter, not having been taught him as an established religion, he examined without fear — and dissented from its inadequacies. The duple system of rhythmical designations, giving adequate representation of only halves, quarters, eighths, etc., was the particular beam in the eye which Henry Cowell endeavored to extricate. He proposed a special notation for other fractions, so as to avoid the annoying and unscientific methods of setting down triplets, quintuplets, etc. This lore, nurtured by Cowell at Stanford University, where he worked as a free lance, was later embodied in a book, *New Musical Resources,* published in 1930 by Knopf. In 1931 Cowell, annoyed by the wistful realization that, no matter what notation we may decree, human players will still be human—that is, inaccurate, physiologically limited, rhythmically crippled, and unwilling to reform—hit upon the idea of an instrument which would faithfully produce all kinds of rhythms and cross-rhythms, as the tempered piano faithfully produces a given intonation for which a player on a string-instrument has to fumble by ear. He spoke to Professor Leon Theremin, builder of acoustical instruments, expounded his ideas, and secured the inventor's valued collaboration. As a result, a new musical wonder, provisionally christened "rhythmicon," was presented to the world for the first time on January 19, 1932, at the New School for Social Research, where Cowell is in charge of musical activities. The rhythmicon can play triplets against quintuplets, or any other combinations up to sixteen notes in a group. The metrical index is associated, in accordance with Henry Cowell's scheme as expounded in *New Musical Resources*, with the corresponding frequence of vibrations. In other words, quintuplets are of necessity sounded on the fifth harmonic, nonuplets on the ninth harmonic, and so forth. A complete chord of sixteen notes presents sixteen rhythmical figures in sixteen harmonics within the range of four octaves. All sixteen notes coincide, with the beginning of each period, thus producing a synthetic harmonic series of tones.

Henry Cowell composed, in 1931, a suite in four movements, for orchestra, entitled "Rhythmicana," in which he treats the new instrument as a sort of rhythmical organ; in one of the movements he amusingly imitates the rhythmicon's effects by building a harmonic scale in wood wind.

Henry Cowell's choices of titles for his compositions are indicative of a scientific spirit which animates him whenever he sets about to solve a musical equation. "Synchrony" (published by Edition Adler in Germany) is a tone-poem for music and dance; its rhythms are quite simple, yet Cowell manages to maintain an air of innovation by such devices as a sudden duplication of the metrical design and by a most ingenious orchestration. In his "Sinfonietta for Chamber Orchestra" he is almost academic, except for the "frictional" use of the interval of a minor second and some unearthly passages for the French horn scaling its harmonic series with little solicitude for the embouchure. In this and similar passages from his other works Cowell is expressive, and it is strange to observe how the two spirits—that of strict science and that of musical expressiveness—achieve a happy symbiosis in Cowell's productions. "Polyphonica," for twelve instruments, is for science, but the suite ("The Banshee," "The Leprechaun," and "The Fairy Bells") "for String and Percussion Piano and Chamber Orchestra," is all for expressiveness, for dynamic and color effects. The first is absolute music, product of a mind that takes nothing for granted; the second is applied music, often with a programmatic title which, however, is always added after the music is completed!

When Cowell is intent on one particular problem, say that of dissonant counterpoint, he deliberately dismisses the wealth of his new musical resources and, by so doing, achieves an unencumbered presentation of the main problem. In the piano "Concerto" (published by Edition Senart of Paris) his problem is sonority, and he uses a full-fledged technique of tone-clusters to the fullest advantage in solo part and orchestra alike. It is easily understood that a tone-cluster in the orchestra is built by simple addition of instruments, and that fifteen instruments, producing single notes, are required to build a two-octave diatonic tone-cluster.

Cowell's titles are usually taken from Celtic lore. The

harmonic scheme in these works (many of them published by Breitkopf and Haertel; we will mention "The Tides of Manaunaun," "Exultation," "The Harp of Life") is surprisingly mild. Indeed, the idiom is so "audaciously conservative" that it is disarming. Cowell was not attempting to revise tonal harmony in these pieces. But in this very unpretentiousness lies their appeal; for, in their primitive directness they draw immediate response from audiences willing to accept the exterior peculiarities of tone-production. The sensational element in Cowell's appearances in both hemispheres does not cancel the fact that, harmonically speaking, many of Cowell's piano pieces are of crystalline simplicity. On the other hand, the sonorous richnesses of cluster music have aroused admiration which Cowell's "scientific" self never seemed to command. Professors of great universities have written exorbitant characterizations of these tone-pictures; and abroad—in England, France, Germany, Poland, and Russia—Cowell's name has become identified with Brobdingnagian sonorities. Cowell went to Russia in 1929; there he was received as a personification of industrial America, with machines governing the tide of life: "And I saw clearly the electric floodlights of Broadway filling the room, and the New York skyline hovering above the mist," wrote a Russian intellectual after a demonstration at the Leningrad Institution of Arts and Sciences.

Henry Cowell edits a unique quarterly publishing ultramodern music, under the title, *New Music*. As publisher, he demands no preconceived qualifications from his composers, and anyone with anything new to say engages his interest. He bars no one except himself—not a note of Cowell's music has been published in Cowell's edition. He specializes on

American composers of the non-conformist type, but welcomes occasional Europeans. He publishes piano pieces, chamber music, and even full scores when finances permit. *New Music* has distribution all over the habitable globe, from Japan over both Americas to all of Europe.

Henry Cowell, in managing various non-lucrative enterprises, is as much of an innovator as he is in composing his own and administering other contemporaries' music. As director of the North American section of the Pan-American Association of Composers, he has organized every activity which this organization has had, including concerts in New York, San Francisco, Havana, Paris, Berlin, Madrid, Vienna, Prague, Budapest, and other places. He works with determination unlessened by the realization that the world, even that part of the world that goes by the name of musical, is little flexible. But Henry Cowell would not be himself if he did not follow the path of most resistance.

Roy Harris

Roy Harris is a curious case among American composers. He is young, in the early thirties; serious, writing in only the larger forms; continually improving his style; deadly earnest, with a devoted sincerity to musical ideals and high standards and with boundless enthusiasm as to his own possibilities.

In spite of these wonderful recommendations, Harris is not as convincing in his actual music as in his musical plans. But this is probably temporary; he has grown continuously, if slowly, over a wide period; the chances are that he may keep on doing so, in which case he will become one of the most important composers we have produced.

Personally, Harris has a plain, driving force, undampable conviction, ruggedness. In his music he reflects some of this. He began by writing in the crudest manner I ever remember seeing from anyone who thought that his products were compositions: unbelievable commonplaces of harmony, like a schoolboy's first exercises; melodic fragments of no distinction; rhythm all half-note blocks in four-four meters. But Harris would point them out with the firm conviction that they were potential masterpieces. It may be noted that this early crudity was due to his having obtained a late start in composing, rather than to lack of native ability.

Today, Harris is not totally changed. He often convinces his friends and listeners of the extreme value of his works by his own indefatigable enthusiasm for them, when in reality they are only mildly interesting and would not be very highly regarded by these selfsame people if they heard them in performance without the stimulating presence of their creator.

That which makes one consider Harris very seriously is his steady progress, unbroken (each work is better than the one preceding), his utter seriousness and sincerity, his constant aim at the highest forms. Also, it would seem that one who has begun with such abject roughness of style, who has had to work furiously to carve out for himself each slightest improvement, whose smallest achievement has meant hard application, may have a chance, through the very knowledge of his foundation which the focusing of his attention on every detail has given him, to advance farther in the end than the composer who has natural facility to too great a degree. This facility often produces laziness in its owner; often he never improves.

To talk with Harris, one would gather that his music must be radical. On hearing the music, one finds it sounding quite conventional. It is not modernistic music. Some elements of it are commonplace enough, so that auditors often lose the genuine originality contained in nearly all his works in their form development. Modernism and originality have been so associated with harmony that if one performs for a sophisticated audience a work with new harmonies it is taken for granted as modern; but if one performs for them a work with old types of harmony but with real innovations in rhythm, form, or even melody, it will be called old-fashioned, and the newer elements will pass unnoticed.

Harris has suffered from this lack of perception. His harmony is apt to be of a familiar sort; once in a while he uses simple polychords effectively, but he is usually content with ordinary triads or secondary seventh-chords with an occasional unusual passing tone. Also, his music is founded, in a certain way, on this commonplace harmony. That is to say, he lacks a natural use of polyphony; what little polyphony there is to be found in his works seems a bit forced, as though he felt the lack of it, and put it in willy-nilly. And even this little counterpoint is based on chords; it is not conceived from the standpoint of melodic line first and harmonic combination second, but the reverse. Such "harmonic" counterpoint he fully believes in and argues for.

Harris' form is based fundamentally on a Beethovenesque concept of thematic developments; but Harris carries the idea onward into new formal developments of his own, and it is in this field that he is truly original, a creator rather than an imitator; yet even here he is conventional, inasmuch as what he does is to apply the Beethoven principles of form, with some additions, to a semi-modern melodic and harmonic idiom. The hopeful thing, from a modernist's standpoint, however, about his classical tendencies is that he is in no sense a neo-classicist. This latter curiosity is a composer who has been a modern in the vanguard, and who later renounces modernism in an attempt to duplicate a bygone style. Harris is naturally conservative musically. He has never been more modern than he is now, but becomes steadily more modern. He does not, in his conservatism, imitate older styles, but creates, through great labor, a self-built style which turns out to resemble in many ways that of a former musical period. He writes music which is original, because he originated it himself, but which is not always new, because many of the things which he originated have been originated long ago by others. All this gives his music a genuineness, however, which is not possessed by many composers who stick to an older idiom, and a strength which no mere imitator could conceivably duplicate.

Harris' methods of developing form are through melodic extension. He often, in development, interpolates notes between thematic notes; but through dynamic accents of the thematic material, the design is clear. Thus rhythm and accent become an essential feature of the formal development. Rhythmic interpolation, as well as melodic, is employed. Placing different tonalities next to each other he finds aids the form. His work is bulky in time and lean in space— that is to say, his type of development demands quite a long time to work itself out, but there is often not very much going on at a given moment—many unison passages, and so forth. Also, even when parts move against each other, they are very frequently in rhythmical unison. He attempts long melodic line, but achieves this often by melodic repetitions. Sequence he abhors. He gains melodic continuity by the typical American method of unequal division of measures (as, for example, dividing a four-four measure into three eighths, four eighths, and one eighth, instead of four eighths and four eighths, the inevitable European way). He also uses an occasional unequal measure, such as seven-eighths, and so forth. This is, of course, familiar in nearly all contemporary music, but Harris is just conservative enough to feel his rhythm to be very advanced on account of these changes, even though he only rarely employs contrasting rhythms against each other. Harris is essentially a tonalist, but believes in an occasional though rather infrequent extension through polytonality. Atonality is too much for him, and actual sound he does not usually consider as a musical element.

In Harris' earlier works, such as the "Sextette" and the "Piano Sonata," he aims for continuous form, but cannot achieve it always, so that the works often "blow up" and the form seems to explode and disappear. In the "Sonata," particularly, he has been influenced by the modern French, and is not at his best, which is his ruggedly American self.

The later works are far more successful. The "Symphony" is quite consistent, although terribly dull harmonically in spots. The "Toccata," for orchestra, a still later work, achieves form and more significant content.

This example, taken from the last movement of Harris' Symphony, shows a group of twenty-eight eighth-notes phrased in four groups of seven notes each, across changing metrical accents. A third element is added to the rhythm by irregular smaller groups within the phrases.

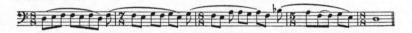

Another bar from the same work shows a typical rhythmic division of a familiar measure of eight eighth-notes into groups of three, two, and three, instead of two groups of four. These examples are very characteristic of his rhythmical employment.

A bar from the "Septet" for wood winds and piano illustrates one of his longest and best melodic lines. There is no repetition, and, although it gives the effect of being quite regular in tonality, the modulations are unusual and original.

68]

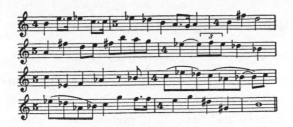

Harris has had important presentations of his chamber music both in America and abroad. He is one of the favored few who have been accorded symphonic performances by our orchestra conductors. The dynamic driving pulse of his music, as well as its ingenuous sincerity and its breadth of scope, places him in the class of the most promising young Anglo-Saxon American composers. His further growth may be watched with eager anticipation.

Wallingford Riegger

According to the general conception, a critic should be a bird of prey that swoops down upon its quarry and devours it piecemeal. Then he will be most feared and the quaking quarry will come to him and beg for mercy and a few kind words. I cannot assume this rôle of a belligerent critic, but I shall try to tell of Riegger as I see him through his music.

I shall not dwell upon Riegger's eclectic propensities. He seems to like canonic and fugal forms. In these days, when the relation of tone to tone is not what it used to be, such titles as canons and fugues no longer impress us as being the scholarly manifestations of composers endowed with super-human learning and technic, as was the case when wigs and ruffles were the style. Riegger uses these forms by force of habit rather than by formal necessity. But in spite of them he strives only to express himself, and this he really does in his best works. The incessant reiteration of canonic forms on the part of composers I can regard only as indicating a lack of imagination enough to find other forms. Though composers have habits which they repeat continuously, these habits might be excused if they are not too obvious. The means of creation, the technic, has always been a secondary consideration with me (except where it is entirely lacking). I speak of it first here to show that Riegger is really not the eclectic professor, but quite a natural though, in certain respects, unusual human being.

The earliest work of Riegger's which I am asked to review

is the "Chromatic Quartet" for strings. It was composed in 1924, not so long ago and yet devoid of Riegger's characteristic marks, with the possible exception of the rhapsodic changes of mood in the slow introduction. The everlasting reiteration of the thematic material in the form of sequences and other banalities makes this an extremely monotonous work. It has the marks of Wagner and Puccini in spiritual content and might sound like good music to an average public because of its sweet, romantic, hypochondriacal expression; but it is not Riegger. The first Allegro theme has a rhythmic, virile quality, but—these sequences! No, the Riegger of the "Chromatic Quartet" is the fettered conservatoirist with many, many complexes and inhibitions.

"Whimsy," a 'cello solo, published by Schirmer in 1930, but composed in 1923, has Debussy's flavor. Attempts at modern writing are obvious, but Riegger does not get any farther than Debussy in this work.

"La Belle Dame sans Merci" (1924) is a musical setting of the poem of John Keats, for two sopranos, contralto, tenor, and eight instruments. I shall pass over this work with the remark that it is the expression of a romantic youth who does not perceive the monotony of his sublime inspiration. There are no contrasting elements in the score.

In "Blue Voyage" the Riegger-ego is beginning to assert itself. Rhapsodic, of Liszt and Ravel flavor, this work expresses nevertheless determination, aggressiveness, mixed with the sentimental expression of a lover seeking his ends. I have never read Conrad Aiken's *Blue Voyage*, but it must be an ethereal, erotic, and, at times, stormy flight if it is anything like this rhapsody for piano, published by Schirmer and composed in 1926. I find the work fragmentary; that is,

I cannot find the relation of all the parts to the whole. Riegger is fond of holding harmonic effects that he likes and juggling them. Glissandos and other theatrical means are not uncommon to his nature. So you see, he is a bit of a showman, though he seems such a quiet, unassuming person.

"Triple Jazz," written in 1923 and revised in 1928, is hardly jazz. It is called "Triple Jazz" because it is written in triple time, three-four time. A touch of humor, which I hold to be Riegger's most characteristic mark, is evident. The hypochondriacal tendencies of romanticism are disappearing. This work should really retain its old name, "An American Polonaise."

With "A Study in Sonority" for ten violins (or any multiple of ten), 1929, the real Riegger comes into being. The work is a splendid example of modern tone-combinations of the homophonic style. The thematic material is not constructed in a definitely closed form, so that one wonders if the composer finishes the idea that he wishes to express. It is not easy to interpret Riegger's personality through this piece. I feel a sort of feline *raffinement,* coupled with grotesque facetiousness. The effect of the music is that of a libidinous tingle in the high registers of the sensory organs. Of course, whatever I say about this work must be wrong to the complex, indefinite, facetious personality that conceived it.

The "Three Canons" for wood winds, 1930, shows better thematic construction. The lines are closed; they are consistent in development; they cadence with a definite feeling for phrasing and articulation. The import of the message is humor, with a dash of resoluteness and of longing.

"Bacchanale" and "Evocation," both 1931, were written

for the dance. I do not like the formal construction of these works. Here we find a concatenation of heterogeneous two-bar phrases which might be suitable for the dance (like the Stravinsky form) but are hardly exemplary of good musical form. The chordal structure of both works is similar; their spiritual content is flamboyant, sensational, self-conscious. I anticipate their success with the public but doubt their musical value. Now follows Riegger's own analysis of his recent work, "Prelude and Fugue":

This is far from being a purely theoretical fugue. Each of the three subjects has been conceived for a particular choir of the orchestra, one being for strings, one for wood winds, and one for brass, an arrangement which, however, does not preclude an occasional shift of rôles. When the fugue is fairly well under way an atonal and many-voiced chorale is announced, phrase by phrase, in the violins—*pianissimo*—while the fugal themes continue their sharply rhythmic progress. After a brief interim the chorale reappears in inverted form, still in the background, played this time by the brass and wood winds, the fugue continuing restlessly in many kinds of stretti. Meanwhile the organ weaves into the polyphonic texture, threading its way among the higher wood winds or lower strings, but not asserting itself positively till near the close, where against the *fortissimo* agitation of the entire orchestra it intones the broad strains of the chorale, overwhelming the warring rhythms of strings, winds, and percussion, as eventually cosmic forces must dominate over humanity's ceaseless striving.

The work is consistently atonal. Wherever possible, color is used to offset the mechanical working out of counterpoint. Thus the second subject (for the wood winds) is itself composed of three parallel moving parts, while at the beginning of the coda (before the final appearance of the chorale) four-part counterpoint becomes the slow contrapuntal movement of four different sets of "chord blocks," each containing four to twelve different tones as follows: horns and cellos four, violins and violas six, organ seven, brass and wood winds twelve.

I have attempted here criticism from a psycho-analytical standpoint, with an occasional regard for technical construction. I confess that this attempt is in no way complete; but I believe that the appreciation and fostering of music would be heightened if our audiences were taught to recognize the living psyche of all works of art.

Roger Sessions

Composers of "absolute music" seldom like to have their personalities obtrude on the music. Roger Sessions writes a music as independent of extra-musical considerations as could be wished. Yet, paradoxically, his music gains in appreciation when it is given a label in space and time—music by an American, written in our time of well-controlled ardors.

Roger Huntington Sessions, though born in Brooklyn, is a New Englander by heritage, temporal residence, and cast of mind. One could go back to Buckle and theorize with him about the influence of the climate on man and his creative propensities. For the "icy flame" of a New Englander seems to have been bestowed upon Roger Sessions at birth. His family history is very instructive; from generation to generation it has been the spirit of secession that animated the Sessionses during the three centuries of their residence on colonial soil. From father to son they have been in the clergy. An irrepressible protestantism, understood in its original sense, must have influenced the progressive sons to secede from the particular denomination of the father, and fall into some interdenominational heresy, down to the present end of the line, Roger Huntington Sessions, a protestant against all denominations and, very likely, against all established religion. The civic spirit in Roger Sessions must have been behind his zero-per-cent Americanism (which, it may be cogently argued, is the true hundred-per-cent Americanism, understood in the progressive sense). He was one of the very few Americans abroad who compromised themselves in the eyes of right-minded people by sending a "protestant" cable to Governor Fuller of Massachusetts in the days of Sacco and Vanzetti. On a previous occasion, when a more personal question was involved, he sacrificed a paying position for the sake of loyalty to a teacher-friend. Of this more anon.

The characteristic circumstance is the fact that Sessions preserves intact the now obsolete sense of personal and civic justice. This, in addition to an innate cosmopolitanism, made him select his residences and friends in a world wider than the one he was born into. He took residence abroad as soon as the opportune Guggenheim Fellowship afforded him a chance. He studied languages with astonishing fervor for a non-professional philologist. Thus he acquired a perfect command of Italian, French, and German. As if this were not enough, he undertook the study of Russian, prompted by the circumstance that several Russian writers and musicians were housed with him at Rome. In this labor of love he achieved extraordinary progress. His letters, in Russian, to this writer are not only grammatical but idiomatic as well, and occasional lapses in the field of Russian conjugations are the only signs of the correspondent's non-Russian birth.

A brief biography of Roger Huntington Sessions follows. Born December 28, 1896. Graduated from Kent School, Kent, Connecticut, in 1911; graduated from Harvard in 1915. The next two years he spent in New Haven studying under Horatio Parker in the Yale School of Music. From 1917 to 1921 he taught composition at Smith College. Sessions met Ernest Bloch in New York, and showed him some of his earliest efforts, among them a symphony. Bloch saw his talent and determination, took him under his guidance, and very soon engaged him as assistant at the Cleveland Institute of Music, of which Bloch was appointed director. In Cleveland, Sessions composed incidental music to the stage play by Leonid Andreev, *The Black Maskers*. The early symphony was definitely relegated to the limbo of perishable juvenilia, but the *Black Maskers* music survived in the form of an orchestral suite, revised and corrected according to the restrained musical philosophy of the later Sessions. For this incidental music to a Russian symbolical play was composed in an emotional, expansive style directly derived from the exalted orchestral imagery of Bloch.

In 1925 Sessions resigned from the faculty of the Cleveland Institute of Music, under circumstances which may be called dramatic. Ernest Bloch was not politic as a chief executive. Enthusiastic in everything that related to his work, he was critically minded in his observations of the matters of management. In a country where arts and sciences are dependent on the good will and munificence of various women's committees and wives of influential husbands, he dared to speak his mind when called upon to make a valedictorian speech, at a function, concerning the policies of the school. As a consequence, he had to resign his position. Roger Sessions did not have to go with him, but resigned in protest against Bloch's dismissal.

There followed his years abroad. In Florence he wrote three chorals for organ, compositions of remarkable austerity, without a trace of the emotional spirit that animated the score of the *Black Maskers*. But what a fine example of saying much with few notes these three chorals are! With this, Sessions begins his search for immanent perfection in correspondence with the particular design of each particular work. He states his profession of faith in these few sentences (1927):

I reject any kind of dogma or platform. I am not trying to write "modern," "American," or "neo-classic" music. I am seeking always and only the coherent and living expression of my musical ideas. . . . . The Flemish and Italian composers of the late XV, XVI and XVII centuries, Bach, the Mozart of "Die Zauberflöte" and the "Requiem" represent to my mind the highest perfection that music has yet reached. . . . . I dislike rhetoric, overemphasis, vulgarity, but at the same time believe that perfection in art consists in a sort of equilibrium which can be neither defined nor counterfeited.

And then:

I have no sympathy with consciously sought originality. I accept my musical ideas without theorizing as to their source or their other than musical meaning.

Sessions' greatest interest lies in the achievement of perfect form. He is almost Aristotelian in his insistence on the importance of the musical "genus." Hence the impression of austerity that the compositions of his mature period produce at first sight. Again, there is that "icy flame" that may be construed as ideal romanticism. Sessions' recognition as a composer resides in these few works written by him while abroad: the "Symphony" (1926–1927), the "Sonata" (1930), and the "Concerto for Violin and Orchestra" (1932). These works, analyzed from the point of view of (1) melody, (2) harmony, and (3) rhythm, reveal the following general design. Melody with Sessions is paramount. In the opening bars of the "Sonata," the cantilena, stripped of almost all detail that is not necessary, rules all supreme. Although he has not written a single composition for the human voice, Sessions derives his art of melody from the idea of a singing voice. This may be the reason why he is so eminently successful in writing slow movements—by far the most difficult art in composition. To give the melody a living shape, he resorts to fractional repetitions of the melodic line, incorporated in the greater melodic design. By this the following is meant: in order to secure a perfect form, the composer employs brief identical figures usually at the end of a period, as a sort of reminiscent quotation, long enough to be recognizable, but sufficiently short not to suggest a recapitulation. It is a device similar to that of terza rima in poetry (as in Dante's *Inferno*), where rhymes follow each other in uninterrupted concatenation.

From the point of view of harmony, Sessions' compositions do not offer any startling revelations. Suffice it to say that he does not pursue the formula vaguely described as "polytonality," but he is unafraid to become harmonically involved if the logical development of separate parts necessitates such a complication of design. *"Warum einfach sein wenn man kann kompliziert sein?"* This ironical query is inapplicable to complications arising from the interweaving of contrapuntal parts in Sessions' works. His counterpoint is neither deliberately simple, nor unintentionally entangled. A remarkable feature is the wise distribution of chromatic material in the main themes. A tonal composer par excellence, Sessions is very liberal in using chromatic deviations in single melody (such as the opening theme of the "Sonata"), but when a fugal development is foreseen (as in the second theme of the "Sonata" and the opening phrase of the trumpet in the "Symphony"), the melodic ingredients are

[79

carefully spaced, usually at thirds ("Sonata"), or fifths and sevenths ("Symphony"), leaving room for future imitations at a second, a fourth, etc. When augmented or diminished intervals are used at the entrance of new voices, the harmony may reach a pretty high degree of saturation, filling the complete series of the diatonic scale, with (if the imitation is done at an altered interval) several chromatic tones into the bargain. The climax, in the form of a tonal impasse, is often presented as an integral tabulation of all elements (a very interesting case of such a climax is exemplified in measures 223–235 of the "Sonata," where — Sessions could not have been unaware of this—even the visual impression betrays climactic tension: there are six staff-lines, of which two are for the sustaining and the loud pedal, respectively).

From the point of view of rhythm, Sessions is as free from extravert complication as he is from apostatic simplification. Again, his choice is governed by the necessity and sufficiency of each particular device. His feeling for form necessitates a general symmetry of the metrical plan. The requirements of phrasing, grouping (if only for the eye), make the time signatures change rather often (particularly in the "Symphony"). When several rhythms are crossed by the bar-line, the accents and special groupings mark heterogeneous rhythms. Very often prime rhythms, such as 5 - 8 or 7 - 8, are but composite measures of three and two units each (which division is always indicated in the score). Among polyrhythmic combinations the favorite with Sessions is the superposition of 2 - 4 and 3 - 8 time. If the general time-signature is 2 - 4, then the 3 - 8 time is indicated by overlapping groupings. There are several interesting examples (in the "Symphony") of interpositions of prime (non-composite)

5 - 8, against 2 - 4. Usually such parallel rhythms are sustained for a very short period (as three bars of 2 - 4 against four bars of 3 - 8).

The "Concerto for Violin and Orchestra" is Sessions' latest composition. It embodies the familiar features of his musical system in a degree which suggests perfection. The slow opening movement, mostly for wood winds (among them the Mozartean F clarinets, now manufactured by Professor Redfield in New York) is remarkable in its sustained song. The scherzo, on the other hand, offers an extremely adroit display of instrumental flashes in quick succession. The solo instrument has the classical cadenza, but outside of this revival there is little ostentatious virtuosity.

Sessions is an ardent student of old music, fonder of Mozart and Verdi than of Beethoven and Wagner. In his music is reflected the direct lightness of the first two rather than the introspective depth of the great dramatizers of music. Stravinsky is moving in the same direction; and, in spite of Sessions' acknowledgment of Stravinsky's influence, it is difficult to discover such an influence beyond a few more or less general rhythmical reminiscences (notably, in the "Symphony"). Sessions has undoubtedly a right to his own place among twentieth-century composers; and the wide recognition of his works, despite their difficulty of idiom and performance, testifies to his worth.

John J. Becker

The Middle West has produced many composers of attainment. In many cases, however, these composers have fled from the Middle West at the earliest possible moment and no longer acknowledge it as their home. Ruth Crawford and Vivian Fine, for example, come from Chicago; now they have both become seasoned Easterners.

The livest composer who still retains the Middle West as his home is John J. Becker. He makes his home not in Chicago, the supposed center of Middle Western activities, but in St. Paul; and such is his energy, and so many and so diversified are his activities, that it is a question if he does not carry the center of interest in modern creative music in the Middle West with him wherever he goes. He composes experimentally, fervently. He is still in the process of building his own musical style, which is forming gradually toward a certain combination of principles of ancient polyphony, not of the Bach but of the Palestrina type, with the dissonant intervals which have come into use in modern times. He aims at independent parts, at development through polyphonic devices, at loftiness, majesty, and at sincere straightforwardness in expression. These objectives he succeeds more and more in attaining with each new work; and his selection of dissonances, always biting and unyielding, becomes more and more resourceful with each new composition.

His earlier works, while showing a modern tendency, are

commonplace. Through experimenting over a period of years, he has little by little replaced the commonplaces with more interesting materials and philosophy. His music never follows conventional lines, either new or old. Perhaps for this reason his work is often very much underestimated. He does not please the conservatives, or even the part-conservatives, as his works are drastically dissonant; he pleases only the more open-minded of the radicals, because his works never follow any particular fads or styles of modern writing. He is, however, becoming recognized on account of his knowledge and technique as well as his staunchness of spirit, both in his personality and in his work.

Aside from his own creative work, Becker is a fighter. He plunges directly into the most conservative quarters and emerges with victory and plunder in the shape of having stimulated new ways of thinking, and openness to new ideas. He works for the most part in Catholic colleges, which, although always emphasizing music, are apt to be extremely conventional. He lectures not for one such college but for many; he travels every week to Duluth; he goes to Milwaukee; he is known throughout the middle Northwest. He tears down moth-eaten conventions, and suggests a different position for all cultural and artistic activities, specializing, of course, on music. He lectures on music and the arts; he conducts orchestral and other concerts of new music in St. Paul and other cities; he writes articles for leading periodicals. The more he is criticized the more grimly he battles. He is a crusader—perhaps the only one among American moderns who could undertake the Herculean labor of overcoming the prejudices of people who are almost entirely ignorant of contemporary arts, and that in a locality where he is quite alone, has not the support of a group who work with him!

If Becker has his way, he will make St. Paul and Minneapolis into leading centers of contemporary culture. And if St. Paul does not hinder him by making him occupy too much of his energy in fighting its doubts, he will war with his personal problems of composition until he takes his place among the leading contemporary composers.

The Rochester Group of American Composers

The American Composers' Orchestral Concerts were inaugurated by the Eastman School of Music of the University of Rochester in May 1925. Originally designed to serve as a laboratory for talented young composers, they have since expanded to include performance and publication of works by well-known composers. In the spring of 1931 these concerts were augmented by the first of a projected series of annual festivals, each consisting of four concerts devoted to American chamber, choral, symphonic, and stage music, providing a brilliant and effective summary of the best work of the past six years.

These concerts have served three essential purposes. First, they have been the means of enabling young composers of technical maturity to hear the first performance of their works without the necessity of submitting them through the regular "commercial" channels. The average symphony orchestra is not financially able to serve as a proving-ground for untried composers. For this reason it is my belief that in the past much promising material remained undiscovered and undeveloped owing to the fact that the obstacle of the "first performance" was never successfully bridged. In the American Concerts it is not necessary for the composer to have a box-office reputation. We are, in fact, more interested in discovering worth-while new talent than in re-performing works of established artists.

Second, these concerts have given performances of both

new and old works of established composers, enabling the hearers to form some estimate of the directions in which American music is moving. The concerts have in this way served as a valuable meeting-ground—an open forum, so to speak—where composers from all sections of the country have come and met together for performances of their own works. (It has not been an uncommon occurrence for every composer represented on a program to be present in person.)

In the third place, the concerts have made it possible to test and retest the value of certain manuscript works which, for commercial reasons, have never achieved publication. We have frequently been able from such works to single out certain individual compositions which have definite program value and have been able to publish them or to arrange for their publication. In the past six years of these concerts we have performed over one hundred works, many of them for the first time, by approximately sixty-five composers. The publications completed to date include two symphonies, five suites, one overture, and three miscellaneous works.

If it is frequently true that an institution is but the lengthened shadow of a man, it is only just to say that in the case of the Rochester American Composers' Concerts the project is the lengthened shadow of a group of men—first, George Eastman, whose idealism made them possible; next, President Rush Rhees of the University of Rochester, without whose enthusiastic co-operation the undertaking could not have been carried on; and, finally, the group of composers belonging to the staff of the Composition Department of the Eastman School of Music. These members of the faculty, all of whom are themselves composers, have provided for this endeavor a background of enthusiasm, loyalty, and co-operation which has been invaluable. It is my privilege here to discuss in as much detail as space permits the individual contributions of these men to American music.

First in seniority comes Edward Royce. Though Mr. Royce did not in point of time actually found the Composition Department of the Eastman School, it may truthfully be said that the department existed only in an embryonic state until his advent to its leadership in 1925. Under his direction the department has grown from one of small numbers to a department which, both in size and in quality of work done, is one of the most useful and vital parts of the Eastman School of Music.

The fact that Mr. Royce is perhaps better known as a teacher than as a composer is due to no lack of creative ability on his part but rather to an enthusiasm for teaching and a selflessness of endeavor that have caused him to sacrifice much time and energy, which might have been used for the furthering of his own interests, to the larger work of preparing a background for the American music of the next generation. This fault, if it be a fault, must be held a very lovable one, and one which, in these days of the self-seeking virtuoso, is rather unusual.

In spite of his passion for teaching, Mr. Royce has nevertheless already contributed to music literature works upon which his reputation as a composer may rest secure. Though he is the author of two notable symphonic poems, "The Fire Bringers" and "Far Ocean," it is in the field of piano music that he is best known. His works for this instrument include the "Variations in A Minor," played repeatedly by Harold Bauer and other eminent artists. "Two Sets of Piano Pieces,"

[87

the last of which is still in manuscript, give further evidence of his mastery of this field.

The latest work from his pen is his "Variations for Organ," which from the standpoint of originality as well as structure seems to me to be the outstanding American contribution to the organ literature of the present century.

Royce's work is characterized essentially by two qualities. In the first place, it evidences a mastery of formal design which is rare in the works of modern composers. The structure of each work, whether it be a small piano piece or a work in large form, is marked by a definiteness of purpose and a faultlessness of design which are unique.

The second quality is a complete avoidance of all sentimentality, a fearlessness of expression combined with high artistic integrity and ruthless self-criticism. This negation of all of the "tricks" of the popular composer, added to the rather stoical directness of his writing, gives to his work a certain acid quality and at the same time impresses the hearer with a sense of strength and inevitability.

The second member of the Rochester group is Bernard Rogers. Mr. Rogers, like Mr. Royce, has contributed through his own individuality as well as through his compositions to the success of the Concerts project. Rogers first came into prominence as an orchestral composer with his symphonic poem, "To the Fallen," played by the New York Philharmonic Orchestra. Since that time he has written a symphony, a symphonic poem, "Adonais," and the "Prelude to Hamlet" for large orchestra; and three works, "Soliloquy," "Pastorale," and "Nocturne," for small orchestra; a string quartet; a work for chorus and orchestra, "The Raising of Lazarus"; and an opera, *The Marriage of Aude.* He is at the present time completing a new choral work based on the Old Testament, "Exodus."

There are two widely diverse elements in Rogers' music both of which must be fully appreciated if his music is to be understood. The first is influenced by an extraordinary sensitiveness to harmonic structure, contrapuntal line, and orchestral color. This characteristic is most clearly perceived in such works as the "Three Compositions for Small Orchestra," in which telling use is made of attenuated line and subtle instrumental coloring, giving the works a certain translucent structure.

In the writer's estimation, however, it was not until the writing of "The Raising of Lazarus" that Rogers attained his full stature as a creative artist. In this work he adds to the technique heretofore indicated a sweep and surge of emotional power that makes the work in my opinion one of the outstanding modern contributions to choral writing. In this work Rogers seems to have lost himself completely in his subject, to have buried technical perfection in the pathos of the material, and to have added to his former sensitive, artistic perceptions a simplicity and a power that are moving.

The opera, *The Marriage of Aude,* follows the choral work chronologically and also to some extent in conception. Over this music also hovers the same melancholy, brooding quality that marks the former work.

The four junior members of the department are Herbert Inch, Gustave Frederic Soderlund, William Ames, and Irvine McHose. Of these four men, all except Mr. Ames received a large part of their training in composition at the Eastman School. Especial interest is centered this year upon the compositions of Mr. Inch, inasmuch as he was chosen by the jury of the American Academy in Rome to be the recipient of this year's Prix de Rome. He is now residing at the American Academy in Rome as a Fellow of the Academy.

Mr. Inch has contributed two works in the orchestral field—a "Set of Variations" for large orchestra, and a "Suite" for small orchestra—and is at present engaged in the completion of a symphony. He has also written a string quartet and a piano quintet.

These last two works indicate a unique contrapuntal talent. This young man, though by no means uninfluenced by the harmonic trend of the day, writes counterpoint as naturally and freely as did the masters of the contrapuntal era. The appearance of a genuine polyphonic talent in an age particularly noted for its harmonic tendencies is worthy of close attention.

Mr. Soderlund, though born in Sweden, has spent his professional life in America and is, both in feeling and in musical tendencies, an American composer. His two best orchestral works, the symphonic poem, "Svithiod," and a "Nocturne," together with a new symphony which he is now writing, nevertheless indicate his Scandinavian ancestry and background. This is evidenced not only in the austere quality of the works but also in the somber grays of his orchestral palette, which he uses effectively.

Mr. Ames has not yet contributed extensively to the orchestral field, but has demonstrated in his piano pieces a high quality of poetic imagery, music perfumed with a strange exoticism.

The last of these young men, Irvine McHose, writes with what I should call a distinctly American flavor. In both his "Violin Sonata" and his "Concerto for Oboe and Orchestra" he has written music that is bright, cheerful, immensely clever, and full of a rhythmic lilt that is ingratiating. In addition to this youthful, sparkling effervescence, his music possesses an innate and infectious sense of humor. Here is another young American who will bear watching.

My own purpose in creating and conducting this series of concerts may perhaps best be explained by a letter written to and published in the *New York Times,* and reproduced in full in the epoch-making book of Daniel Gregory Mason, *Tune In, America:*

Composition is the most important thing in music, and the composer is the hub of the musical wheel. Mr. Offandonsky could not startle audiences with his magnificent reading of the Beethoven *Fifth* if there had not been Mr. Beethoven to write it! In spite of the obviousness of this fact I have been amazed to find that intelligent people were devoting their chief thought to the performer rather than to the creator.

As the composer is of prime importance in music, so is the national composer important in the development of a national musical culture. The development of the "Russian school" is of recent enough date to serve as a striking example. There is no reason to believe that the United States is an exception to this general law of development, nor is there any reason to believe that we shall develop our own music except by the same intense concentration upon our own composers.

It is not possible for one man, no matter how great he may be, to produce a significant national development. Such a development must be the work of many composers. Some of these men will have great talent and some will be of lesser talent, but it will be the combined efforts of all these men that will be fruitful.

It is equally imperative to foster spiritual atmosphere that is favorable to creation. In other words, the subsoil must also be tilled so that we develop among those interested in music a feeling of interest in and sympathy toward creation. I believe that this is a matter of the greatest importance. It is a problem of back-breaking difficulty for a composer, no matter how great his talent, to attempt to express himself if he is living in an atmosphere where his fellowmen and -women have no interest in or sympathy toward what he is doing and do not consider that it would be important even if he should produce a masterpiece! I believe that even a Beethoven might conceivably be frustrated in such an environment.

These concerts have been generally attended by the composers whose works were performed, and out of this has come an important and rather unexpected development. Composers from all over the country have gathered together from time to time and have come to know each other. They have discussed their problems and their philosophies of music and in doing so have developed a sympathetic understanding of one another. They have found that the American composer is trying to do a distinctive piece of work in expressing through music the life of his own country. This resulted in a certain consolidation of purpose, a sort of communism of artistic endeavor, which has been very thrilling for me to watch.

The festival of American music which we have just concluded called forth from the entire faculty and the student body the greatest zeal and enthusiasm. It is impossible to live in the midst of such an atmosphere without feeling its stimulus and essential productivity.

Henry Brant

Of all very young composers in America, Henry Brant, the Jewish-Canadian American, has the most original things to say and the most perfect technique for saying them. He lives in New York, and at the present writing is eighteen years old. When he was still sixteen he wrote his "Variations for Four Instruments." No more perfect examples of modern counterpoint come from our best composers. It would be impossible to discover the age of the composer from the music. There are many remarkable things about the "Variations." The first point that strikes the examiner of this score is the fact that Brant had a definite idea, and that he carried it out precisely, without yielding to outside influences.

It is remarkable that one of Brant's age should deliberately and openly abjure the question whether or not his music sounds well. Some composers try to be ill-sounding; this is quite another matter. Brant does not mind if the "Variations" happen to sound well. But the point of the "Variations" is something altogether different: they are a rigidly intellectual working-out of a fine musical scheme. It is also wonderful that Brant should have the courage to be deliberately intellectual; "intellectual" music is in very bad repute, even among people who should know better and who admire intelligence in other fields.

The idea which Brant has carried out in the "Variations" is the result of examining musical resources clearly, with a mathematician's mind as well as a musician's ear. By doing

[93

this, he came across an idea which should have occurred to theorists long ago but which as far as I have been able to find out is entirely original. The idea is to create harmonic relations obliquely, instead of vertically. To understand this, we must point out the familiar way of looking at harmony as the vertical relationship between notes one on top of another, and melody as the relationship between notes following one another horizontally. So far, then, we have only two ways of looking at musical sound—either straight up and down, or sidewise. Brant discovered that one could profitably utilize the relationships of tones in oblique positions to each other, as for example, between the bass of one chord, the tenor in the chord following, the alto in the third chord, and the soprano in the fourth chord, this whole relationship being considered as an "oblique harmony." This is a crude illustration. Since there are infinitely many different oblique angles to be constructed within the right angle of the vertical and horizontal lines, there are correspondingly infinitely many possible relationships to be discerned by considering music from this point of view. A world of exploration is opened up by the idea. The only precedent it has is in either fugue form or canon, in which each voice enters with some specified relation to a past note in another voice. But a canon is childishly simple from the oblique standpoint, since if the relationship of a canon in the unison is considered, the second voice of the canon always follows with just the same melody as the first, so that the oblique relation will always remain a unison instead of one of different intervals. In Brant's "Variations" the idea of oblique harmony is carried out, and one oblique harmony resolves into another. The actual effect of this procedure, to the ear which does not know how to listen, is polyphony. The polyphony which results is extremely good; but Brant wishes the oblique harmony to become evident to the persons to whom his work is presented. The music must be heard, as that is the purpose of it; but as so few "get" the oblique harmony on first hearing, or by hearing alone, he requests that each auditor be supplied with the written score and watch the music while it is being played. So the music is to be heard and seen simultaneously. Under no circumstances, according to the wish of the composer, is it to be seen without being heard or heard without being seen! This is a new concept invented by Brant to solve the difficulty of presenting his intellectual musical concepts to average musicians.

Besides oblique harmony, the "Variations" contain an original form; and original form is very rare! The "Variations" are for four voices, and there are four themes upon which variations are made. These four themes are all announced simultaneously, one in each voice, at the very beginning, in counterpoint against each other. Afterwards, every bit of melody in any of the parts is built out of these four themes. There is no free material added. Very few composers have moral courage to continue such a scheme; most of them succumb to the voluptuousness of adding free parts or pretty-sounding harmonies. Another original point of the "Variations" is that the four voices are not assigned to any four particular instruments, as is done in practically all music. Brant directs that the work be played by any instruments with contrasting tone-qualities. Contrasting rather than the usual blending tone-qualities are necessary to bring out the independence of each individual part. But since the interest in the piece lies in the music itself rather than in the orchestration, any suitable group of instruments may be used.

In his "Two Sarabandes" for piano, two very short pieces in two-part counterpoint, the same sort of independence and elegance of each line is preserved. In order that no one line may come out at the expense of the other, and because the interest in the works is in the melodies and counterpoint, not in dynamics, he directs that they be played with absolute evenness, without expression, without ritard, accelerando, crescendo, or diminuendo.

All these examples illustrate his way of thinking and show how original his approach is and how fearlessly he takes any necessary step, no matter how unpopular, to preserve the inherent ideas in his works. Some of his other music which I have not mentioned is very expressive from the conventional standpoint. He does not always write in one manner. But his compositions nearly all contain fresh ideas which do not come from outside influences. They are original with him, and he has had to fight absolute misunderstanding from nearly all the musicians with whom he came in contact. His instructors have been very conventional, and have told him that he was only stupidly imitating Stravinsky by trying to write "modern" music. Brant knows far better than his teachers that Stravinsky's style is entirely different from his own.

Brant is a musician with knowledge, technique, original ideas, feeling, something to say, and courage. Nothing is too great to expect from him in the future, although at the moment he is experimenting in merely clever music.

Howard Hanson

Among the growing number to whom the concept "American Music" has a meaning, some are interested mainly in composing, some in colorful personalities, some in scholarship or technique, some in education, some in organization and nation-wide co-operation, and some in orchestras and conducting. The one American known to this writer who is of impressive stature and commanding importance in every one of these departments is Howard Hanson. Barely to name a few of the achievements and activities of Dr. Hanson gives a picture of versatility and vitality in which America may take pride musically as well as nationally. He has composed *Beowulf,* "The Romantic Symphony," "Pan and the Priest." He is founder and conductor of the American Composers' Concerts at Rochester, and director of the Eastman School of Music, where he teaches in one of the most significant all-American composition departments in our land. His work as president of the Music Teachers' National Association of Schools of Music and in other activities of the sort has a beneficent influence greater than any one person or even institution can wield.

Whether one judges Hanson's composing from the standpoint of vitality, that of originality, that of interesting content, that of appropriateness, or that of emotional intensity, he challenges attention. But beauty dwells in all this music. By beauty is meant not mere loveliness, which is also often present, but the sheer urge and exaltation due to a happy combination of any or all of the more elementary qualities

[97

first named. *Beowulf,* for example, a choral work with orchestral accompaniment, expresses the lament of a nation for a dead hero. The starkly primitive ancient Saxon effect of William Morris' words rings through the setting. It is pathetic, thrilling, and immensely powerful. It is inexorable, granitic. One other choral work of recent (more recent!) times is comparable to it but does not in any way surpass it; that work is Stravinsky's "Symphony of Psalms."

Other works of great strength and beauty, of approximately the same period, are the "Nordic Symphony," "Lux Aeterna," "Pan and the Priest," "North and West," "The Organ Concerto," and a string quartet.

Mr. F. Morris Class, himself a noteworthy American composer, once remarked to this writer: "Say what you will, not one of us has yet struck instantaneously the note of beauty, as Tschaikowsky did at the opening of the B Flat Piano Concerto." But Mr. Class said that ten years ago, and is now answered by Hanson's "Romantic Symphony." This work, with all the energy and vigor, the sure grasp of the varied harmonic and orchestral palette of the modernist already evident in the composer's earlier works, has also an idyllic, a haunting quality that sets it apart from them. And as, with the title "Variations Sérieuses," Mendelssohn protested against current conceptions of frivolity in a great musical form, so Hanson protests against the mode of belittling anything in the least beautiful by calling it "romantic." For if that which warms the heart, from the "Carnival" to "L'Après-Midi d'un Faune," is "romantic" then Hanson's "Romantic Symphony" need not blush at its title.

If Hanson were nothing but a composer, his work would still be a powerful argument that America has reached her musical majority, surpassing as it does all but a very few of the outstanding European works of recent years. But Hanson has also answered the question, "Which is better, co-operation or competition?" His answer of course is "Both," and is given in a very practical way by five American Composers' Concerts which take place each year in Kilbourn Hall, in Rochester. At these concerts about one hundred American works, by about sixty-five composers, have been played during the last seven years, some several times. Composers of all ages, from Loeffler and the late George Chadwick to Herbert Inch, have contributed. The public interest in this project is intense. Hundreds are turned away from each concert. The performances are often equal in quality to those of the best-known symphony orchestras and surpass in number of American works given those in the entire country elsewhere combined. This series was initiated as a sort of composers' laboratory to give beginners and amateurs a chance to experiment and to hear their works. But the quality of pieces submitted has improved so rapidly that this object, while still in itself unchanged, has been supplemented by another—to afford all fine works of outstanding American composers a steady opportunity of being heard. As yet no other project remotely comparable to this exists in America or other countries. In their day, Liszt and Rimsky-Korsakoff were famous for helping their fellow-composers. But neither of them conducted year in and year out a series of concerts for this end alone. Incidentally Dr. Hanson is one of the most brilliant conductors of modern music.

In addition to his work as composer and as "conductor-promotor" Hanson is director of the Eastman School of Music in Rochester. Under his leadership this school, a branch of the University of Rochester, has developed into a strong and in some ways unique force for good in American musical affairs. Owing to his sure instinct for selecting men whose technique and personality fit them for their special tasks, and his patience and thoroughness in conducting conferences, the instrumental departments have become outstanding, the student orchestra is a splendid ensemble, and the ear-training is actually taught, not merely printed in the catalogue. All the major theory teachers are themselves composers, many of them graduates of the school. The composition department, after employing foreign teachers of reputation, who were uniformly unsuccessful, upon Dr. Hanson's advent was thoroughly Americanized with gratifying results. Two or three complete programs (one for orchestra) of student compositions are played each year. Training in traditional harmony and Bach counterpoint forms a basis for sane modernism. The course in modern harmony given by Dr. Hanson himself is in reality a laboratory course in advanced composition.

Meanwhile Hanson's efforts in behalf of co-ordination of educational resources in America and his attempts to convince bewildered and deracinated foreign conductors that (a) they are employed in America, (b) they are musically employed in America, (c) there is American music, and therefore (d) it should perhaps not be an altogether unheard-of procedure for them at times to play American music to Americans, are tireless and unceasing.

The points at which Hanson touches American musical civilization, and touches it effectively, are so numerous that, while it is difficult to tell what he is to us all, it is almost easier than to discover what he is not.

100]

Carlos Salzedo

Carlos Salzedo is a French Basque*who has made America his home for many years. An unparalleled harpist, his chief contribution to composition has been his use of the harp in many new ways. By experiment, he discovered well over a hundred precise and differentiated types of tone possible to obtain from the harp which were either previously entirely undiscovered or were used by chance quite casually by other players.

These possibilities are all unified and woven together in his "Concerto for Harp and Wood Winds," which contains new excitement and joy at each turn of the page. It gives the auditor the exhilaration of hearing a steady stream of novel and genuinely musical sounds in a composition which is scored in a masterly manner, and is clever and brilliant throughout. This is a piece of music which has interest quite outside of its array of unusual harp sounds. It is witty and deft, and a delightful relief from the over-ponderousness of some schools of modern composition. Salzedo's general style is built on that of the modern French, but the much diversified palette of harp sounds gives it a piquant flavor of its own. He is an innovator who is at the same time an excellent general musician.

*The ascription of Basque origin to Salzedo was a mistake.

Carlos Chávez—Mexican Composer

It is strange that, though Carlos Chávez is twenty-eight and has lived in New York for the last few years, and though he has composed a considerable amount of music, he should still remain unheralded among us. His name is familiar only to the small inner circle of forward-looking musicians who formerly frequented concerts of the International Composers' Guild. Even there, his performances were few and his music never received extended comment. For all that, Chávez does not have the air of a misunderstood genius. He seems able to bide his time, and with good reason, for the value of his music cannot be impaired by lack of immediate recognition.

Carlos Chávez is one of the best examples I know of a thoroughly contemporary composer. Without consciously attempting to be "modern," his music indubitably succeeds in belonging to our own age. This is so not merely because he can on occasion contrive intricate rhythms, or because he prefers linear to vertical writing, or because he composes ballets rather than operas. These things alone do not constitute modern music. But Chávez is essentially of our own day because he uses his composer's gift for the expression of objective beauty of universal significance rather than as a mere means of self-expression. Composing to him is a natural function, like eating or sleeping. His music is not a substitute for living but a manifestation of life. It exemplifies the complete overthrow of nineteenth-century Germanic ideals which tyrannized over music for more than a hundred

years. It propounds no problems, no metaphysics. Chávez'
music is extraordinarily healthy; it is clear and clean-sound-
ing, without shadows or softness. Here is absolute music if
ever there was any.

Carlos Chávez is a Mexican—that is to say, he is a native
of a country virtually without composers, without organized
orchestras, without even a musical season. No tradition of
art-music exists there: the Mexican musician of serious in-
tentions is entirely submerged in the imported European
product. These are formidable obstacles in the path of a
young composer. That Chávez should have been able, in
spite of conditions so unfavorable, to create a markedly
individual style is a feat in itself, but that his music should
be recognizably that of a Mexican is hardly credible.

Yet, there was nothing precocious about the development
of Chávez. His apprentice years were spent in Mexico City,
where he was born. A sister began teaching him to play the
piano at the age of eleven, but he was never willing to accept
a teacher in harmony or counterpoint. He read the theory
books for himself, compared them critically, re-examined the
truth or falsity of their rules. With the autodidact's instinct,
he accepted nothing on hearsay. Even today he uses his own
simplified version of the conventionalized sign of the treble
clef—a small point, but indicative of his independent nature.

Chávez himself feels that he learned to compose principally by analyzing the works of the classic masters. Using
these as models, he had already, before the age of twenty-one,
produced a considerable number of works. A year later, in
1921, he composed his first Mexican ballet, "The New Fire."
It was the first time he had looked away from Europe and
turned to the vital forces of his own country for inspiration.

The composer himself did not comprehend the full import of this until some years later, but from that time he had really found his way.

Mexico possesses a rich fund of indigenous musical material in the ritualistic music of the Mexican Indian. Little known even in Mexico, it is difficult to hear this music, and it has never been taken seriously by the professional musicians of the country. Chávez had visited the Indians each year, and was steeped in their music long before he consciously thought of it as a basis for his own work.

It is easy enough to create a national school of music with the aid of folk-melodies. One simply incorporates them in an opera or a symphonic poem. But this essentially mechanical process seldom proves satisfactory. There is a certain incongruity inherent in the attempt to place simple, popular themes in sophisticated harmonic settings, and it is even more difficult to build with them a large and compact symphonic edifice. It was in the last century that the "Russian Five" first introduced nationalism in music by this method. Since that time all racial minorities have adopted it as a means of asserting their musical independence.

Chávez, in "The New Fire," wished to do likewise. His use of Indian themes in this first essay was too literal. Their treatment, compared to what he has since achieved, resembled the rather inorganic manner in which Manuel de Falla has employed Spanish themes in his ballets. Chávez' next composition, however, "Three Sonatinas," for violin and piano, 'cello and piano, and piano solo, written after an interval of three years, shows a considerable improvement. The piano "Sonatina" is the most characteristic of the group. It is refreshing, original music with a kind of hard charm and a distinctly Mexican flavor. No Indian melodies are actually quoted in this "Sonatina"—Chávez had begun to rethink the material so that only its essence remained. Here and there a recognizably Mexican turn of phrase can be discerned, but as a whole the folk-element has been replaced by a more subtle sense of national characteristics. As Debussy and Ravel reflected the clarity, the delicacy, the wit, and the formal design of the French spirit, so Chávez had learned to write music which caught the spirit of Mexico—its sun-filled, naïve, Latin soul. With extraordinary intuition, he has, in fact, in his more recent work, combined the two kinds of nationalism represented respectively by the French and the Russian schools. Thus, single-handed, he has created a tradition which no future Mexican composer can afford to ignore. If I stress this point, it is because I feel that no other composer who has used folk-material—not even Bela Bartok or de Falla—has more successfully solved the problem of its complete amalgamation into an art-form.

Chávez' second Mexican ballet, *The Four Suns,* based on an Aztec legend, is one of his most delightful works. It is made up of simple, clear-cut rhythms, which lend the whole composition a very definite and inevitable aspect. This fresh, vital music has its roots so firmly in an ancient culture that, at times, it takes on something of the monotony of the Indian dances themselves. Two works for small ensemble are "Energia," for nine instruments, and "H.P., Dance of Men and Machines." The latter was heard in New York, but cannot be counted among Chávez' best work. A delightful sense of humor is displayed in his "Three Hexagons," for voice and small ensemble, and in his small piano piece, "36." It is mordant, dry humor without a trace of irony or malice.

Undoubtedly, his most mature work to date is a recently completed "Piano Sonata" in four movements. This "Sonata" gives a confused impression on first hearing, because of the individual technique with which it is put together. It seems to contain a profusion of short melodic germs, none of which is developed in the usual manner, so that a sense of incoherency is created. This is produced also by the fact that the style is very contrapuntal; the separate voices move in such a way as to produce a judicious mixture of sharp dissonances and sudden bright unisons. Add to this a special kind of piano writing—thin, hard, without lushness of timbre—and it is clear that this work presents formidable difficulties to even the sympathetic listener. But familiarity with the "Sonata" convinces me that in these four highly condensed movements, each one of which seems packed with meaning, Chávez has put the best of his genius. They contain a personal quality which it is impossible to describe in words, yet constituting his chief claim to originality.

Chávez, of course, has his limitations—limitations of scope, possibly of form and of melody. Nevertheless, he is one of the few American musicians about whom we can say that he is more than a reflection of Europe. We in the United States who have long desired musical autonomy can best appreciate the full measure of his achievement. We cannot, like Chávez, borrow from a rich, melodic source or lose ourselves in an ancient civilization, but we can be stimulated and instructed by his example. Of Chávez it may already be said that his work presents itself as one of the first authentic signs of a new world with its own new music.

Nicolas Slonimsky

Slonimsky, originally Russian, has adopted America both legally and artistically. He is effervescent, exhilarating, heady, ever-energetic. After a very few years in America, he learned more about the English language than natives know, and he now triumphantly informs his poor, unenlightened English-speaking friends how to better their conversation. His literary products are accepted by *Disques,* the *American Mercury,* the *Boston Transcript,* and other publications.

Slonimsky composes, but composition is not his main interest. He is author, conductor, lecturer, pianist, accompanist, and a myriad of other things besides.

Nevertheless it would be a great mistake to suppose that Slonimsky has contributed nothing to contemporary composition. He receives much criticism because of the light nature of his works. This giddiness, however, is his much-prized specialty! Where others pompously assail the depths and heights, arriving at bombastic conclusions, Slonimsky sophisticatedly aims to glitter—to please for the moment, to be clever, amusing. And he succeeds! His music is always delightfully witty, even in his little "pot-boilers," of which many are published. Although these works do not transcend the commonplace in material, they always have a clever notion of some sort to carry them through, usually programmatic. His humor is always partly textual, but there is also genuine satire in the music itself. His "Studies in Black and White" will relieve the funereal aspect of any modern program; his settings of well-known advertisements to song are classics. In his only orchestral work up to the present he depicts a game of chess, carefully working out the moves and gambits in realistic musical motives which need no explanation. When the melody moves from C to F, and then slithers to the side to F sharp, one knows it represents no other than the famous crooked knight's move!

Behind Slonimsky's deliberate and carefully sustained shallowness, however, there are serious and valuable musical ideas. If we take his "Studies in Black and White" as a typical example, we find the ingenious technical device of having one hand play (on the piano) all white keys, the other hand all black. This is not without relation to the musical form itself, as it must be admitted that the technique of musical composition for the most part rests on the technical possibilities of instruments. The result of dividing the hands in this way on the piano is not only a new and enticing way of playing the instrument, but induces a new sort of crossing of the parts in wide skips in such fashion that what at first glance appears to be utterly commonplace assumes an altogether new character, owing to the voice leading. It is a new polyphonic way of looking at very familiar material.

The other new aspect of the "Studies in Black and White" is the use (in all the early ones) of nothing but literal concords—no seconds or sevenths are permitted, even in passing. This is a daring and radical step. No composer in modern times has presumed to be so utterly concordant! But Slonimsky goes even farther: he makes the music sound dissonant through the modern use of cross-relation and atonality. His concords are not, therefore, used as were concords in ancient times; and the works are far from being a reversion to the old. On the other hand, they give the impression of modernity through continual cross-relation of rapidly moving concords, and his works are examples of something very rare—a new use of old materials. With this is combined the idea of a counterpoint in "mutually exclusive tonal systems," each part moving along its own scale (diatonic and pentatonic in this particular case).

Outside of his composition, Slonimsky has done great service to American music as a whole through having produced and conducted more works by original Americans than almost any other conductor in his concerts with the Boston Chamber Orchestra, and for the Pan-American Association of Composers through America and Europe.

Ruth Crawford

Descended, as very few of our American composers are, from exclusively Anglo-Saxon stock, Ruth Crawford grew up in that traditional cradle of Americanism, a minister's household. She was first educated as a pianist in Chicago and did her harmony and counterpoint with Adolf Weidig. Encouraged by Djane Lavoie-Herz and Dane Rudhyar, she turned the corner toward modern music and in 1929 bravely burned her ships behind her, following what may have become almost a slogan in some parts of the country: "Young woman, go East." After a summer at the MacDowell colony in New Hampshire and a year in New York, a Guggenheim Fellowship, the first given to a woman for musical composition, took her to Europe.

The style of her work before 1930 is basically homophonic, not too noticeably of the Scriabin school, but embroidered with sudden whirls and whip-snaps of thirty-second notes that give a distinct and characteristic vitality to what is often a languid moodiness in the basic chordal structure. These vicious little stabs of dissonance remind one of the lion's tails in the movies of the African veldt. As an integral part of a more mature technique the device becomes handled most successfully in the ironic setting of "Rat Riddles" ("Three Songs," 1930–32),* where the piano and the oboe chase each other around in the most surprising arabesques to a percussion accompaniment, the two instruments and the

* Words by Carl Sandburg.

voice and percussion giving the impression—such is the independence of parts—of a whole small orchestra, busily engaged in a contrapuntal tutti. Upon the gay irregularity of the fabric of these instruments, as *concertanti,* has been superimposed a slow and solemn orchestral *ostinato* of a purely percussive character, whose regular tread makes a very unusual effect—a counterpoint between two groups, one in florid counterpoint, the other independently homophonic.

The third song, "In Tall Grass," is executed along similar lines—the same instruments *concertanti* in much the same texture but the *ostinati* divided into two groups, strings and wind, giving a repetition, not of a tonal, but of a dynamic pattern, the strings a faster, the wind a slower one. All three of these songs are comparatively heterophonic. By *complete* heterophony we understand a polyphony in which there is no relation between the parts except mere proximity in time-space, beginning and ending, within hearing of each other, at more or less the same time: each should have its own tonal and rhythmic system and these should be mutually exclusive, while the forms should be utterly diverse. Heterophony may be accidental, as, for instance, a radio-reception of Beethoven's "Eroica" intruded upon by a phonograph record of a Javanese gamelan. But from an artistic point of view, a high degree of organization is necessary (1) to assure perfect non-coincidence and (2) to make the undertaking as a whole worth while.

The basic principle ("together-soundingness" in which "separate-soundingness" predominates) can be applied in a modified way, as in these songs, of which the second one, "Prayers of Steel," is the most heterophonic. Tonally, all the parts (except the percussion) use the duodecuple gamut, but with practically no unisons, or, indeed, any apparent chordal structures between them. Rhythmically, there is regular, planned coincidence of beat and accent, based upon persistent repetitions of five diverse metrical patterns. The basic poly-metrical (rhythmic-chordal) complex, rigid and severe, may be represented as follows:

This four-part structure is presented three times by the *concertanti,* the third containing an extension of one measure. After a measure's rest the whole is given *da capo,* making twenty-eight measures in all. The fifth part is presented by the *ostinati* in double octaves and has, instead of a repetitive, a cumulative pattern, given four times in the total of twenty-eight measures, but in four different versions:

The initial tone of each *gruppetto* presents, transposed at a major third and in metrical augmentation, the first phrase of the oboe part. This oboe part is built upon an initial "set" of seven tones. In the first two-measure phrase this is presented five times, the accented tones which mark off the five sets being, in consecutive order, the first five tones of the initial set, the remaining tones in each set following in their original order:

The second two-measure phrase has the same scheme except that the whole business is transposed upon the second tone of the initial set. The third, fourth, fifth, and sixth two-measure phrases are similarly constructed and each is transposed upon the third, fourth, fifth, and sixth tones, respectively, of the initial set. Less than a dozen liberties (shifting and substituting of tones), taken to avoid the "hitting of unisons" between parts, are the only departures from this outline. The voice part is the only rhythmically free part. Tonally, it is centered rigidly upon G sharp.

Similar methods of organization abound in other compositions by Miss Crawford, as, for instance, in the third movement of the "Suite for Solo Flute," a little *passacaglia* with the pattern 7 - 7 - 7, and in the last movement of the "First String Quartet" which has a pattern (10 - 10) + (10 - 10)′ + 10 followed by a cancrizans, one-half tone higher, 10 + (10 - 10)′ + (10 - 10) . . . . . .

Most listeners and even readers of this music are not aware of the joyous play of the intellect in it. The smoothly rippling and carefree though enigmatic line in no way betrays, though it is absolutely dependent upon, the strict logic of the structure. When not informed beforehand, people sometimes say Miss Crawford is going impressionist. When informed, however briefly, they charge her with being intellectual. Now, the music is the same in either case, is it not? It can be analyzed so as to show a "reason" for every note, or listened to in entire dependence upon the aesthetic effect alone. Serious music must be capable of submission to both tests. It is a co-operation of head and heart, of feeling and thinking. The trouble with so much modern music is that there is a fight on between the two—the head is afraid to think and the heart cannot feel, or vice versa. Composers, take notice! Romantic music would have died a natural death twenty years ago. It is kept alive only by the artificial respiration administered by non-musical agencies—endowed schools, churches, and business. To keep it from growing out of their control these institutions encourage the fallacy that music is primarily or exclusively concerned with the emotions. Too many composers are deceived by this propaganda. Great art cannot be built upon feeling alone or upon feeling primarily. "Gefühl ist *nicht* alles!" Without more adventurous and fundamental thinking and better social and technical orientation, even feeling gets tangled, and stays tangled. Neo-classicism, neo-Romanticism, and other misnomers are mere conscience-quieters for workers in a pampered art who are at their wits' ends for a compass, a course, and a hand at the helm.

There are also successful experiments in the balance of phrases of such measure-lengths as the following outline of the last movement of the flute suite:

4 - 5 - 4 - 5
7 - 7
2 - 2 - 2

By the modeling of the line, the structure can be clearly appreciated upon a first hearing. While eminently practicable for performance, the organization of the phraseology is only too likely to be missed by performers of the present day, accustomed, as most of them are, to plunging in, "getting the notes," and not much else, consequently bewildering even the most attentive listener. By "modeling the line" is meant proper distribution of primary, secondary, and tertiary accents, breathing-spaces, dynamics, and rubato; and, above all, the clean-cut execution of similar, continuant, and opposed phrases in such ways that they are actually felt by the listener as similar, continuant, or opposed.

The most ambitious work is a string quartet in four movements (1931). The first movement is rhapsodic in character, though the structure is thematic. The second and last movements are characteristically whip-snappy, fast movements—the latter consists for its second half in an exact cancrizans in all four parts of the first half. The third movement is the most remarkable, an experiment in dynamic counterpoint. Each part has a different alternation of crescendo and diminuendo or else the same alternation but beginning and ending at different times. The tone-pitches are homophonic, sometimes in very close spacing (seconds and thirds), and sometimes very wide. We look forward to the hearing of this unique step in the widening of our technical resources.

Miss Crawford is now engaged upon the task of writing her first work for large orchestra. It is to be in two movements, the first in three voices—a kind of Toccata-Allegro, with broad lines to the very independent parts, and the second, another experiment in *passacaglia* form, but this time of a chordal, rather than a melodic, unit.

The problem of form is, for her as for all of us, the crucial one. Her last year's work shows in this all-important branch an increase in sureness of what she is about and a resourcefulness in going about it that are most gratifying. The attention to the various factors entering into the composer's work is unusually well distributed. Especially in respect to rhythm we may note a variety of invention scarcely to be seen in the work of any other composer.

We are, then, in a fair way to be able to answer the common question regarding the occurrence among women composers of any who stand out beyond the rank and file of male epigones. Miss Crawford certainly does. In fact, one can find only a few men among American composers who are as uncompromisingly and successfully radical. Not the least refreshing thing about her work is the absence of pretense. Quite sure of the sort of stuff she wishes to write, she is wise in not attempting the grand, the pompous, and the showy. This indicates also a quality that will be taken for a weakness by many concert-goers in America as well as in Europe. Men composers have so accustomed us to musical rhetoric during the last century or so that it must take quite a little courage not to fall in with the honored traditions of fanfares and splurges of orchestral color, with a lot of orchestral players working hard and long. Her works are invariably shorter than one thinks they will be. Yet when they have ended, one recognizes that, as in the case of Carl Ruggles' "Angels," one has heard something that most men would have spun out to ten times the length—and missed.

Still, in all art, the sensational, the strong bid for attention, nay, the sheer commanding of it, has a legitimate place. Showmanship does count! Many composers have this quality without having anything else but a bag of tricks. They are the ones whose names appear much upon concert programs while they live—and never afterward. But all the great composers, too, have had this sense of showmanship. It is part of the paradox of art—especially, of music—that one can never tell when the artist is not "putting it over" on one. Goethe has a nice way of stating the situation: there are three kinds of art, the playful, the serious, and a third kind in which both playfulness and seriousness are blended; the first two are manner; the last, style. Showmanship, at its best, is exactly this last. At its worst, it is mere play; but at its best, such a blending of seriousness and play that one does not know or care which is which. It may be play but, damn it, one is deeply moved, as well to thought as to feeling.

This quality of showmanship is reputed to be much prized by Americans. It has, on the whole, distinguished American art by its absence. Some of the younger men in American music are cultivating it; and with success. But we have a long way to go before we can be much of a match for the Europeans. Most audiences and most music-lovers are lazy. They will not stir an inch to get something that is good for them. They must be literally knocked on the head, bludgeoned into giving attention. It is here that the jazz-writers have stolen a march upon their more serious colleagues. It is an error for the serious ones to imitate the stuff turned out by the playful ones, but they should emulate more the *attitude*

[117

toward the audience, the *skill in manner of presentation*, and the *adroitness* in reaping large rewards, shown by the vastly over-rated playboys. Of course, the romantically minded will retort something to the effect that the serious artist is rewarded by posterity. Surely he is; but that is no reason why he cannot be rewarded now, too. In fact, we have a notion he will be rewarded all the better by posterity if he is a good showman.

Of course it is refreshing every now and then to come across someone who absolutely refuses to put on a show. We surely need in music a splitting up of the field of composition. It is absurd to expect all composers to write for the same audience and absurd to expect one and the same audience to appreciate all music. There must be music for the many and music for the few—quite a number of distinct musics for various fews. Music such as Miss Crawford's could very well find a permanent place in a small repertoire of an intellectual sort for a particular group of people who were interested in that sort of thing. Eric Satie was not widely known, but he had a profound influence upon the history of music.

The next few years will decide whether this most promising young woman will rest content in the rather narrow, but recherché, field in which she has hitherto moved and had her being, or whether, following her bid for orchestral laurels, she will enter into the already brisk competition among men in the larger fields.

Charles Seeger

Charles Seeger is the greatest musical explorer in intellectual fields which America has produced, the greatest experimental musicologist. Ever fascinated by intricacies, he has solved more problems of modern musical theory, and suggested more fruitful pathways for musical composition (some of which have proved of great general import), than any other three men. He has rarely been given public credit for the ideas which he has initiated, since with a perverse humor which is very characteristic of him he always presents his important new ideas in such a way, at such a time, or to such people that they are never accepted at first; later when the ideas have proved to be singularly adaptable, their users often forget the source.

While Seeger has worked out some of his findings himself, his greatest importance lies in his subtle influence in suggesting to others both a new musical point of view and specific usages in composition. Few modern composers, either in America or abroad, are entirely uninfluenced by him; yet most of those who use his ideas do not know his name and believe themselves to have originated the ideas, so delicately does he work! He has a new idea—he imparts the idea to a few important acquaintances, usually in such a way as to cause instant repulsion on their part and to irritate them greatly; but Seeger does not mind irritating: he knows that if he irritates his subject enough, the idea will be remembered, and passed on. And this is what actually happens. He springs an idea which is so unpopular and unprecedented as

[119

to cause absolute outrage, in California. One of the insulted listeners, who travels a great deal, goes to Germany, and in an aggrieved manner relates the idea, perhaps as an example of idiocy. Next season a new and unprecedented type of music will be shown to the world by a young German composer. So it has gone. He not only has no credit but often has to fight against personal irritations which he has sometimes aroused through his methods of presentation, in people who do not understand his witty but cynical way of getting results.

He is personally a bundle of contradictions; but where a majority of people are self-contradictory without suspecting themselves of it, he knows it of himself and is satisfied! All his vagaries are quite self-conscious. He is outstandingly (and to many people obnoxiously) intellectual, but with a leaning toward sentimental outpouring. Here again he sees the tendency in himself plainly, but instead of frowning on it as a thing to be hidden, he takes prankish delight in it. He is rigidly conservative in many ways, never accepting thoroughly anything until it has been entirely proved, believing in precedent, training, even bookishness. Yet no one else has taken as great an interest in the new, the unexplored, the modern. He is aristocrat and radical, but nothing between.

As a composer Seeger has produced little, but all he has produced is of importance in the history of indigenous development in America. From the standpoint of precedent, one must concede to him the position of being the second in time to create works which are genuinely dissonant from beginning to end, and which in other respects are thoroughly experimental. The first is Ives, who started quite independently on such explorations about 1897. I have no knowledge of anyone else before Seeger, who, about 1912, broke away from the imitative style of his early songs and began a series of nervy experiments which resulted in his "Parthenia" music for two public productions at the Greek Theatre in Berkeley. A veritable wealth of examples of fantastic dissonances, curious rhythms, new melodic structure, and form, are to be found in these works, to say nothing of the orchestration! A germination bed for musical ideas. They are, however, not focused; they are scattered, and do not stand up as musical compositions. After their creation, Seeger became so self-critical that it was for many years virtually impossible for him to complete a work. He has discarded music which almost any composer in the world would have been proud of, because of some infinitesimal fault which no one but he himself would have knowledge enough to mark. Thus the intellectualism which is one of his predominating features became so rigid as to quench the creative spark; that is, almost. Not quite.

During this period he composed a few works, which he will never show, and pretends he does not have. These works are short, and are all but absolute perfection. Nothing in music surpasses, for instance, his "Solo for Clarinet" in exquisite delicacy, in beauty of tracery, in unity of idea, in unbelievably developed melodic line. It is far more than an intellectual experiment. It is great music! It is an etched cameo, and in it he completely eradicated the fault of his earlier music, which was to try out too many things at once!

To return to Seeger's ideas. It may be asked, What are some of them with which he has influenced composers?

When the whole world thought Stravinsky and Schoenberg both insane, Seeger found them the most important new composers of their time. They were. He at that time, when the average musician could see no difference between the two, predicted that Stravinsky would become popular with the general concert public and that Schoenberg would be beloved by musical intellectuals. This has come to pass. Before Schoenberg eschewed thickness of sound and wrote the economically outlined "Pierrot Lunaire," Seeger worked for the downfall of over-voluptuousness and a return to thin lines of music. This at a time when, under the influence of Strauss, music was thought to be good inasmuch as it was full and thick, and to call music thin was to damn it utterly. Now the return to thin line has penetrated every circle of composers.

At a time when Debussian impressionism was the rage, Seeger advocated sharp definiteness of line. Now this definiteness is attempted by nearly everyone, and impressionism has all but disappeared. Before the idea of piling one chord on top of another as being the only line of musical development had lost its sway, Seeger suggested a return to counterpoint. The return has been made. Before Hindemith produced his works in dissonant counterpoint poured into a Bach mold, Seeger suggested this very idea, and created a system for such a counterpoint, worked out to the last detail of what the intervals should be and how they might move. Hindemith and Schoenberg both came out later with works embodying the principles of Seeger's suggestions. Long before Stravinsky supposedly led his group of followers into "neo-classicism," Seeger predicted the whole development of this return, or attempted return.

At a time when it was generally considered unaesthetic to

use unresolved dissonances, Seeger predicted that in a very short time all possible dissonances would be freely used throughout all new music. They are. Away back, Seeger insisted on being enthusiastic about very ancient music; no one could see what possible musical value it had. Seeger also pointed out that it has similarity with modern music, in point of view; at that time no one could see the resemblance —people as a whole saw modernism as a "bunch of discords" only. Today, nearly all modernists have developed an interest in very old music, and the relationship between the very old and the very new is recognized.

Seeger pointed out the possibility of analyzing certain modern complexes as polychords, long before the word was generally known. He has often taken special interest in the works of certain composers who at the time were relatively unheard of, and insisted on his students studying them. A few years later, there has invariably been a wave of public interest in the direction of these composers. Monteverdi, Bruckner, and Stravinsky are examples.

One could go on indefinitely and not exhaust the number of subjects in which he has been a pioneer. Probably his most important standpoint, however, is his open advocacy of the intellectual point of view in approaching music. This he started at a time when such a thing was utterly inconceivable —when it was considered that music had value only if it had nothing to do with the intellect, that the most damning thing that could be said against music was that it is intellectual, and that *thinking* about music not only has no value but destroys the musical impulse. Seeger almost proved this old-fashioned notion to be right by allowing over-intellectualism to stultify him. But he has brilliantly recovered, and has renewed activity in a great new outburst of fertility. And, as in the other cases, the public is gradually following him in this, his most important stand. There has been a reaction against "sentimentality," against gushing; a movement which is gaining strength is openly opposed to "expression" as the aim of music (Seeger suggested this long ago). Although the name intellectualism is still in bad repute in musical circles, actual intellectualism is in full power. The very ones who rant against intellectualism are the most eager to discuss music, to talk about it. This very attitude, of course, denotes the intellectual approach. So things are going his way; but paradoxically (he is always paradoxical) he also strongly advocates not talking so much about music, but letting it talk for itself. The intellectual elements which he most admires are those contained within the materials of the music itself, not so much questions concerning the philosophy of music.

Seeger has always advocated an interest in "musicology," or the study of all things pertaining to music scientifically. His latest activity is the editing of the new edition called *American Library of Musicology.*

How long will it be before the lethargic musical public learns the ecstasies of investigating this alluring field?

Walter Piston

Walter Piston owes his patronymic to his grandfather, Pistone, an Italian by birth. The final "e" fell off when Pistone came to America; he married an American woman, and his son, Walter Piston's father, married an American.

Piston was born in Rockland, Maine, on January 20, 1894. His childhood and early youth were spent without indication that he was to become a musician. Other interests occupied his time; he went to an art school in Boston, and after graduation entered upon the career of an artist. He studied violin and piano mostly as a sideline. He did not go to college to study music but became interested in it from an intellectual point of view. For himself and by himself he tried to establish the fundamental musical laws.

He played the violin in the Pierian Sodality, which is the University Orchestra of Harvard. Later he became its conductor, and studied instruments and the technique of orchestral scoring.

At that time he was already proficient in theory and practice of composition. He attacked the large forms at once, and wrote for the orchestra. Following in the footsteps of many an American composer, he went to the Conservatory of Fontainebleau to study with Nadia Boulanger; and upon his return he was well qualified to join the Harvard Music Faculty when the opportunity came. He has written a scholarly volume on harmony, shortly to be published.

Perhaps the most significant work of Piston is his orchestral "Suite," performed by Stokowski at the all-American broadcast in the spring of 1932. The composer appears in it a full-fledged modernist. The old system of tonality all but breaks down in this score; Piston desperately fights the tonic-dominant complex; and to avoid fifths and octaves suggestive of tonality, he builds his themes on the augmented fourth and the major seventh, these two banners of the dodecuple system. He acknowledges the fascination which the formula holds for him; but he does not join out-and-out atonalists in cultivating the rigid schemes of the Vienna school; rather his atonality is an escape from the musical past. The fugue of the third movement of the "Suite" is built on a motive of three notes, with interval-indices, the major seventh, the augmented fourth, and the perfect fourth (which latter is the difference between the first two). It is instructive to observe that the perfect fourth is treated by Piston as a tetrachord, always tonally.

The "Suite" is an American work, and Piston is nothing loth to incorporate a "blues" interlude in the score. "Snare-drum with wire brush" marks the four-four time, and the crooning melody is woven against it in the best manner of symphonic Broadway.

Walter Piston is one of the most frugal composers, even in New England; Sessions is only second to him. But what little Piston writes invariably finds its way to public performance. His is not a hedonistic music, yet it is human and playable.

The "Sonata for Flute and Piano" enjoys particular favor among the sponsors of advanced chamber music; then there is the charming "Triphony for Flute, Clarinet, and Bassoon." The "Suite for Oboe and Piano," in five divisions, commands

126]

easy attention in view of the paucity of material for this combination. The "Sonata for Pianoforte" and the rather obsolescent "Symphonic Piece" (a sort of absolute music with a vengeance) complete the catalogue of Piston's acknowledgeable works.

Among American composers, Walter Piston appears as a builder of a future academic style, taking this definition without any derogatory implications. There are composers who draw on folklore, and there are composers who seek new colors, new rhythms, and new harmonies. Walter Piston codifies rather than invents. His imagination supplies him with excellent ideas, and out of this material he builds his music, without words, descriptive titles, and literature. He is an American composer speaking the international idiom of absolute music.

Charles E. Ives

Charles E. Ives is the father of indigenous American art-music, and at the same time is in the vanguard of the most forward-looking and experimental composers of today.

Many composers before Ives tried to utilize American folk-material; such men as Stephen Foster practically composed folk-songs. But some of their music yielded to banal European influences, because they invariably altered the original rhythms (often fascinatingly irregular) so as to fit the current European mode, which was nothing but 2 - 4, 3 - 4, 4 - 4, or 6 - 8 meter, and in note-lengths nothing but whole, half-, quarter-, eighth-, sixteenth-, or thirty-second notes, or, at the wildest, eighth-note triplets. Also, all the slight deviations of pitch in the musical scale of the American village folk, wrought in deepest musical ecstasy, were (and still are by most arranger-butchers) altered so as to suit the conventional European mode of tuning of the major or minor scales. And, perhaps worst of all, a schoolbook harmonization like a hymn in four-part harmony was given to all alike. Thus the process of squeezing out all the original life and fire of the music was complete.

Ives was born in 1874 in a small Connecticut town where native music lived. His father, a musician, conductor of the band and experimental enough to be interested in acoustics, was evidently a splendid influence. He did not try to narrow down or standardize the views of his son, but allowed him to hear all the native music in its charming and naïve entirety, and encouraged him to think for himself. This led into a scientific-musical understanding, and to the ability to sort and utilize his many impressions and to build from them a new musical structure. Such a structure is what Ives has created.

As a child, Ives heard the village band. Not all the members played exactly together; there was always a player or so a fraction either ahead or behind the rest. The pitch of the notes was not always the same with all the instruments; some played a bit sharp, some a bit flat. Sometimes the bass tuba would be an indistinguishable pitch, almost a percussion noise. Perhaps the trumpet, or rather the cornet, would feel jolly enough to play his addition to the whole quite independently, so that his part would be altogether different from the rest of the orchestra; yet he would eventually find a way to get in with "the bunch."

Or perhaps Ives heard the fiddling to a dance. The fiddler not only did not play in tune with the conventional notion—he did not want to, and it would have been wrong if he had. His idea of music was quite different, and through slips and slides, and slightly off-pitch tones, which could go loosely under the title of "quarter-tones," he created the right and proper music for the village dance. Kreisler and Heifetz are masters of their art, yet neither one of them could play the fiddle in an old American dance. They would not know where to accent, where to "dip" and "pull" the tone, where to be deliberately and joyfully "off-tune"! The old village fiddler is as much master of his craft as they, although neither can excel in the system of the other.

Ives was also influenced by the village church music. With a wheezy and often out-of-tune-to-the-point-of-discord

[129

harmonium playing simple hymn concords as a base, the congregation sang soulfully and nebulously around the supposed tones of the tune. The so-called unmusical of the congregation sang along behind the tune in both rhythm and pitch, either a bit flat or those with great self-assurance over-aiming at the note and sharping on the high pitches! And in the hands of some of the organists, the harmonium would sometimes play the tonic chord through a passage where the dominant tones were sung in the hymn, or vice versa. Yet the singing was intense in feeling, as well as spontaneous.

Such native characteristics exist all through American village and country music. They are typically American, and are the distinctions between American folk-music and the folk-music of the Europeans from which we spring. Yet the "cultivated" musicians who collected and published these songs of our people unconsciously and without question weeded out all such irregularities and the result was that there is not the slightest suspicion of an original, indigenous, or truly American feeling left in the published versions of these songs. The sad part is, also, that the village children in the schools have learned the songs from the notes, and sing them in the narrow, stiff way they are written down, losing all the native beauty and charm of the unwritten variations, the fine spirit of minstrelsy in the songs and dances. The children naturally take for granted that their elders sing badly and that the notes taught in school are correct; whereas the truth is that the notes are a miserable and vain attempt to preserve the living art of the older folk. Thus the spontaneous way of folk-singing is being rapidly lost.

All of the elements of back-country New England music were assimilated by Ives, on whom they made a deep impression. Having too good a musical ear and general perception to do as the others have done and remove in the cultivated version of this music all the characteristic and charming irregularities, Ives began early to build himself a music in which he could include all these mooted elements. Working with musical feeling deeply rooted in the spirit of the music rather than from a purely intellectual point of view, he found that it was necessary to build his whole musical structure from the ground up. It was impossible for him to confine himself to the known scale, harmony, and rhythm systems brought from Europe.

He therefore found it essential to form a new and broader musical architecture, a scheme of things which, founded on American folk-music, permitted the use of all the elements to be found in it. He did not discard any elements of known musical culture (except irrelevant pedantry); all of them are present in his work; but he also included the extra-European elements of the folk-music as actually performed, and made a new solid foundation on this music, which permits infinite development and cultivation. With breadth of concept, and beginning from the rock-bottom of American soil, he proceeded to write one work after another, each one going farther than the last; and through feeling rather than a mechanically thought-out plan he created an individual musical style. This style contains an astonishing number of elements to be found in no other music. In the end, the music goes far from its folk-foundation into symphonic works of length and complexity. As Burbank created a world of unsuspected optical beauties in flowers by the selection and cultivation of undeveloped tendencies in plants, so Ives took apparently slight elements of American folk-music, and by diligence and sympathetic cultivation found new musical beauty.

The style of his finest music is a style of richness and outpouring, of warmth and largesse. It is humanitarianism applied to sound. No element of music, no matter how unpopular, is left uninvited—all possible elements are included, and not only included but made warmly welcome in the musical fabric. It is a music not of exclusion but of inclusion, and is the most universal in its use of different materials and shades of feeling of any music which I have ever heard. Ives is a wizard at taking seemingly irreconcilable elements and weaving them together into a unity of purpose and flow, joining them by a feeling of cohesion, as well as through the logic of his system, which, as I have indicated before, is wide enough to bring together elements of many different sorts. In the hands of many, such free combinations would result in a hodgepodge; with Ives they result in grand music. There is great similarity, artistically, between Ives and Walt Whitman.

To try to give in words an impression of the feeling of any music is futile—one must hear the music itself. Let it suffice to say that Ives's music contains endless shades of profundity and ecstasy, humor and sadness, commonness and exquisiteness. That which can with more interest be spoken of lies in the analysis of the means used and a survey of what actually takes place in the music.

As a beginning toward an analytical understanding of Ives's works, one must take into consideration his point of view. He believes in music as a vehicle of expression, not so much a personal expression of himself, the composer (although this is included also), but a general human expression. He regards a musical composition almost as though it were a living organism, of which the composer gives the germ, the performer adding to its growth by widening the initial concept. For this reason, although there are always certain delicately balanced sounds about which he is very particular, he gives the performer unusual freedom in playing his works. He does not believe in laying down an absolutely rigid pattern for performers to follow, but believes that if the performer is great and adds his creative fire to the composer's in the rendition of the work, new and unexpected beauties will be born and the concept of the work will grow and flourish. This view has made it difficult for Ives to find the best way of writing down his music. There are always passages which he feels may be played in any of several different ways, depending upon who the performer is and how he feels at the moment, without injury to the composition, since the composition is a germ idea which may develop in any of a number of different directions. Therefore, if he writes down one certain way, he fears that the form of the piece will become crystallized, and that players will fail to see the other possibilities. This idea has led him to pay particular attention to the manner of writing down works, and has resulted in a number of characteristic features of his scores. For instance, he gives directions in a certain place for the performer to play very loud if his feelings have been worked up sufficiently; if not, he is to continue playing more softly. Very frequently, also, he gives a choice of measures. When the player comes to a certain place, he chooses between two or three different measures, according to how he feels. The same idea is also carried out in individual notes: there will be very full chords written, with a footnote stating that, if the player wishes, he may leave out certain notes or, if he wishes, he may add still more! In many places it is indicated that certain measures may be left out at will. In other places, measures are given which may be added at will. In still other places, certain parts may be repeated at will. Many other similar and characteristic directions may be found.

The same fear of hampering the freedom or cramping the feelings of the performer has resulted in his creating very independent parts for each of the men in his orchestral works. Each player, with a very strong feeling for the general whole, has his own quite individual part. The result is a full polyphony, as each one is apt to have his own melody, and all may be sounded together; yet the whole synchronizes into a rich unity of sound. Individual players are often rhythmically independent also, and are asked to play a different rhythm of their own across entirely different rhythms of the rest of the orchestra, but coming out together with the rest at some specified point! In several instances he writes for two orchestras at once, each playing something different —different in harmony, melody, and rhythm. Sometimes they come out together; but I remember one case in which one of the orchestras ends somewhere in the middle, and the other goes on, the winner of the contest. The second orchestra is requested to play, not in a certain specified cross-rhythm against the main orchestra, but in an independent rhythm having nothing to do with the other; and it is indicated that they may find themselves ending anywhere within several pages in relation to the main body of the music, which is taken by the "first" orchestra. This idea came from hearing two bands passing each other on the march, each playing a different piece. Ives was marching with one of the bands;

consequently the other seemed to rise in strength as it came near, and die away as it drew further away.

A good example of the Ivesian individual-part writing is in the latter part of "Washington's Birthday," in which the orchestra changes from an Allegro to a slow movement. The viola, however, is still full of the feeling of the Allegro, so continues to play an altered version of it against the rest of the orchestra's Adagio! In the same work, in the Allegro, the flute-player feels that the tempo should be faster; so he plays it faster than the rest of the men, and his measures come out a sixteenth-note shorter than those of the rest of the orchestra on this account. One can find such examples throughout Ives's music.

Ives notates many things which are unusual and not to be found in any other music, together with some things which are very common in performance, but which it is unconventional to write down. An instance of this is shown in his "Concord Sonata," in which he writes six whole notes and a quarter-rest in 7 - 4 meter. This indicates the actual length of each tone, which is to be held over with the pedal, one note overlapping another. This is very frequent in practice, but I know of no other instance of its being notated. Ives recognizes, as I have said before, that the notated form of music is only a skeleton about which the performer wraps the flesh and blood of the living being of the composition. Ives does not, however, believe in presenting in the written form only the cut-and-dried conventional outline. He believes, probably quite rightly, that this form of notation does not in the least stimulate the imagination of the performer into finding the subtle deviations which give real life and character to the music. Ives tries to induce the performer to share in the creation of the work he is playing by showing, in the written-down form, one way of really performing the piece, carefully worked out, and written down as nearly as possible in the way it actually sounds. This has led him into placing on paper rhythms which are sometimes actually performed but which have never been seen on paper before. From this as a beginning, he also developed rhythms which have never been used before but which he found ways of writing down.

Similarly, in melody, if he wished to suggest the feeling of a country fiddler who plays music with scales tuned unconventionally, he did not write down the tones of our scale which are close and let it go at that, but attempted to write down the exact shades of pitch. This increased his interest in quarter-tones and other intervals of less than a half-step which are to be found in many of his works. In the same way he wrote down the actual lengths of tones held by the pedal. Writing down a scale with the pedal held, he found that all the tones of the scale had to be written as a chord. Such a chord had never been seen on paper before, and was a great sensation; yet similar chords are actually sounded by every pedaler of Chopin. Seeing these chords on paper led to their use later as a new and independent sort of harmony. Ives has also taken special interest in refinements of tone-quality, in which he desires certain overtones to come out, and in delicacies of dynamics, which he puts down with care.

Thus his original notations cover all known fields of musical materials and are in themselves an indication of his covering of all fields, of his musically overflowing in every conceivable direction, of the wealth and fertility of his invention.

An analysis of some actual examples will give a clue to the

style which he has developed, the materials he uses, and the way he has of fusing into a musical and emotional unity the riff-raff of cheap, discarded musical materials, the complete gamut of materials in good general standing, and the innumerable materials which he has personally added to the world's palette of possibilities.

All the developments which will be shown in the examples here are original with Ives, not influenced by other composers. Ives attended practically no concerts whatsoever at the time that he was developing his materials and style, and certainly none in which "modern" usages were shown; also it must be truthfully said that Ives in some of his works came before his more famous European contemporaries, Schoenberg and Stravinsky, in the use of materials which they are credited with having been the first to use. Not that they were influenced by him, of course. They had no more heard of him than he of them. Apparently it was the right time for such things to develop, and they sprang from several sources almost simultaneously. In any case, Schoenberg began writing in the dissonant style that made him famous in 1909, and the first completed works were made public in 1910. It was at the same time that Stravinsky threw off the shackles and branched out independently.

Ives began using experimental materials in his music about 1895. At first they were more or less impressionistically employed—the sound of drums by sounding a number of bass notes together on the piano, or the impression of two bands playing at once through playing chords in different keys together, and by using at least two rhythms at once. But gradually the sounds thus conceived became more and more interesting to Ives as a musical medium in themselves,

and he used them to wider advantage. Tone-clusters, poly-
harmonies, polyrhythms, strong dissonance, atonal passages,
rapid metric change, jazz-rhythms, and many other materials
supposedly dating from a later period were freely used by
Ives between 1895 and 1907, and then were further developed
until about 1916 or 1917. Before the twentieth century these
materials were utilized by him tentatively and occasionally;
from about 1901 onward they became a fundamental part
of his style. All his larger works were written before he
had ever seen or heard any music by either Stravinsky or
Schoenberg.

Sometimes his findings are surprisingly similar to those
invented later by others; sometimes they are in directions not
yet explored by others but which will unquestionably be further utilized in the future, as they are inevitable in the line
of historical musical development.

The bar below shows the sort of ejaculatory rhythm for
which Stravinsky later became famous, a rhythm of off-beats
sharply accented, with the same dissonant harmony always
continued. These things are shown perfectly in the excerpt
from "Putnam's Camp," written long before.

The next example shows a sort of syncopation and accent
which is associated with jazz, a type of rhythm which has
only very recently been adopted in "serious" music, and
which has been considered to be original in jazz. It is a

138]

recent mode in the orchestral works of Gershwin, Copland, and Gruenberg. Roy Harris in his article speaks of such rhythms as characteristically American; that he is right is all the more proved by Ives's use of them in his symphonic work, "Second Orchestral Set," near the beginning of the century. The jazz part of this set was written about 1902 or 1903.

Specially characteristic of Ives is the remarkable rhythm scheme in these bars from "The Housatonic at Stockbridge." Such a rhythmical fabric as is shown here is not an unusual case, but the sort of thing that is to be found throughout Ives's music. It is an interwoven texture of rhythm. Rhythms

[139

are used against each other at the same time, forming harmony of rhythms in the same way that tones are used together to make the more familiar harmony of sound. Just why the idea of a harmony of rhythm has remained practically undeveloped with us, or why there has been so much prejudice against the idea of different simultaneous rhythms, is very hard to say. They sound magnificent, and are in current use among all peoples of the world, with the sole exception of the conventional music of Europe. In Ives's works such different rhythmical harmonies are very varied, and it can be said with certainty that nowhere in the world have such rhythms ever been written down before. Ives goes farther in rhythmical development than any other composer either of today or of yesterday. In the measures on the opposite page one finds as a rhythm-harmony different parts moving simultaneously in 20, 17, 8, and 5 notes to the measure, with other parts in figures taken from rhythms of 12, 10, 6, and 4 to the measure. It is specially notable that Ives's use of cross-rhythms is through long experience so free that one seldom finds a simple underlying rhythm mechanically thumped out on every beat. The rhythms are all or in part varied by means of figures or patterns within the realm of each rhythm-system, and by means of accents and phrasing. With anyone else, a rhythm of 17 against 20, for instance (if one could find anyone else audacious enough to go that far!), would mean 20 against 17 equal and unvaried notes. In the example shown, the 17-rhythm is varied by the second and third note being tied together; the 20-rhythm also has the second and third notes tied, and is divided into groups accented in tens. The accent does not fall on the first beat of the 20 but on the third note before the measure. The

group of ten notes goes through the bar-line, so that the
eighth note after the bar is again the accented note; then

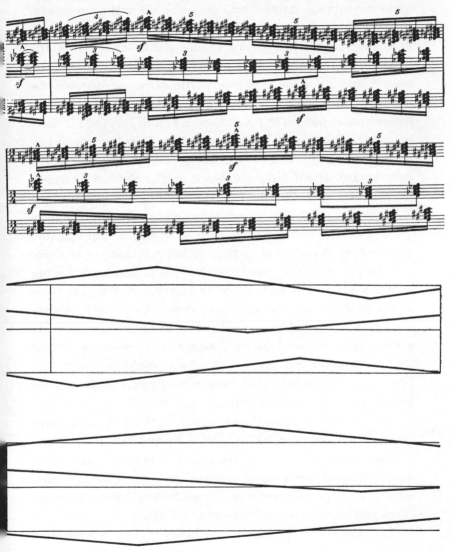

another ten; then three notes before the end of the measure falls the last accent; and so forth. Such schemes give enormous rhythmical interest and diversity. It will be seen also that the rhythm of eight is divided into fours, and that the first note of the four-group is one eighth-note before the bar-line, so that the fourth and eighth eighth-notes are accented, instead of the first and fourth, as would otherwise be the case. This way of straddling the groups across the bar-line is now to be seen in much music; before Ives used it there is hardly an example to be found. I have heard of one or two isolated instances, but no one has ever been able to tell me just where! It will also be seen how the rhythm of five is phrased in two's, again across the bar-line.

Such a rhythm-polyphony makes a polyphonic style absolutely essential in the sound also. It would be hard to find greater polyphonic freedom than in the combination of melodies in Ives's works; yet there is also a harmonic feeling which binds all his melodic parts together and makes them sound almost homophonic. It is evidently necessary in a style so diversified both rhythmically and melodically that there should be a strong harmonic unity. Otherwise the whole structure would fall apart, and chaos would be the result. Ives's style has a powerful harmonic surge, and sounds far less complex than it looks on paper.

The graph (p. 141) shows melodic lines in counterpoint against each other for the first violin, second violin, and viola.

Ives has developed "polyharmony" very strongly; one finds chords of contrasting tone-systems placed against each other even in his very early works of the late 1890's. In many cases polychords are used one after the other.

Ives was the first to make any extensive use of tone-clusters, or harmonies built on major and minor seconds instead of thirds as in the conventional system. Example 4 shows an instance of how he has employed such clusters of tones in running chord progressions along scale lines, in such a manner that there is always a different set of actual intervals (that is, a different relationship between the major and minor seconds within the cluster) in each successive cluster. There are three sets of clusters, each in a different key system, so that one also has an example of polytonality. There are seven tones used in each cluster, making twenty-one different independent parts! Yet they are made quite clear by the simplicity of the outlines. Each of the three cluster-lines has an independent rhythm and melodic curve. The counterpoint of these curves against each other is shown in the graph following the example. Such clusters are used for many measures in "The Fourth of July," as an accompaniment figure, and are considered as lines of sound. Sound itself, as being a musical element no less important than melody, harmony, and rhythm, is an important view of Ives. Musicians often stupidly assume that the same written note must always mean the same thing, forgetting that in our way of writing music the same note is often used to indicate many different sorts of sound.

Melodically, Ives also has something unusual to say. With true courage, he is not afraid to utilize melodies so simple that other modernists shun them; or, on the other hand, to use occasionally some very complex melodic structure. Such a melodic structure is seen in the development of the theme E flat, D flat, C, B flat, B, C in the "Second Pianoforte Sonata." The variations are made by widening the distance between the notes into different octaves. In the final form, a span of five octaves is reached! A truly pianistic idea, as the piano is the only instrument on which tones so separated hang together melodically. One can follow the melody perfectly in this instance. Like atonality, this idea of using wide melodic skips, usually credited to Schoenberg, was used first by Ives.

Countless other examples could be given of things which have been developed by Ives, as his fecundity seems never to be exhausted; but perhaps those already given will serve to show the many different directions in which Ives has experimented farther than any other composer, and in directions which he has found either before other composers or at the same time quite independently. I hope I have shown also that an interest in materials as such is not his main interest. His finding so many new musical resources is the result of his powerful musicality, which demands freedom of expression. He is not content, like many superficial radicals, with merely tearing down known standards. If Ives finds it necessary to reject an older standard, he never rests until he has created a new structure to take its place. Such creations he has made and still makes in every field of music, and the result is a wonderfully universal, rounded-out whole, not technical, but deliciously and fascinatingly human and charming, and with an emotional but not a sentimental basis.

Recently, Ives has had very favorable reviews from some of the world's most famous critics, and is beginning to come into the recognition he so richly deserves. Yet as a whole, particularly formerly, he has been subjected to absurd misunderstanding and stupid criticism. If he wrote four whole notes in 4 - 4 meter because he wanted each tone held a whole note with the pedal on the piano, musicians would ask whether he knew the difference between a whole note and a quarter-note. He was snickered at because he suggested that a row of tone-clusters should be played on the piano with a board of certain length and properly cushioned, for the reason that there are too many notes in the cluster to play with the fingers. Perhaps because they were not practiced enough to play them, musicians laughed also at his rhythms without making the slightest attempt to examine them earnestly and to find out what was really meant by them. More recent criticisms have also sometimes been equally superficial. It is complained that his texture is too thick. That is, of course, because the style, now, is to have thin music. There is no reason why music should not also develop in richness. Those who believe in rigidly fixing every note, in making an absolutely exact and crystallized form for music, complain of his minstrel-like qualities and of the freedom he permits his interpreters; yet there is no reason to suppose that music will not develop in freedom as well as in precision. Again, it is complained that in his orchestration certain parts will not "come out." These parts are not meant to come out, but to alter slightly and delicately the color of the tone, an acoustical flavoring!

All these criticisms are due to the fact that some of the aspects of music which Ives has developed are momentarily out of style. Many of these aspects, however, are now growing into general recognition, and one can predict that his work will come more and more into public favor. Public favor comes slowly to those great enough to be independent. Ives is independent, and is truly great; both in invention and in spirit he is one of the leading men America has produced in any field.

COMPOSERS IN DISCUSSION OF
GENERAL TENDENCIES

Problems of American Composers

America is vast and elemental; America is desperately struggling to wrest social balance from her omnivorous industrialism. America is rolling plains, wind-swept prairies, gaunt deserts, rugged mountains, forests of giant redwoods and pines, lonely rockbound shores, seas of wheat and corn stretching on to the elastic horizon, cotton and tobacco fields, fruit orchards, little bare mining towns huddled on the sides of mountains, lumber camps, oil fields, and New England mill towns. America is smoking, jostling, clamorous cities of steel and glass and electricity dominating human destinies.

America is a nightmare of feverish struggling, a graveyard of suppressed human impulses; America waits calmly between the Pacific and the Atlantic while the tide of the Mississippi rises and falls with the seasons. Our land waits for us clothed in the elements and the vegetation which rises to meet them; our people, our society, are as spiritually naked as the pastoral Indian society which we conquered.

Wonderful, young, sinewy, timorous, browbeaten, eager, gullible American society, living in a land of grandeur, dignity, and untold beauty, is slowly kneading consistent racial character from the sifted flour of experience and the sweat of racial destiny. Slowly, surely, there are emerging American types, with characteristic statures, facial expressions, and temperament.

Those of you who have been in Europe know that the characteristic American cannot avoid identification. It makes

[149

little difference whether he came from the Western plains or from an Atlantic seaboard city; on the Parisian boulevards or among the Swiss Alps, in the English theaters or in Florentine galleries, he is immediately recognizable as an American. He has no poise, he is searching for something, he is concerned about his destiny and the appraisal of his people and his country, he is willing and eager to discuss homely social philosophy with you, he is naïvely receptive and easily browbeaten and yet he radiates a fresh vitality, an unlimited reserve of energy; one feels within him a reticent ego which dares not emerge yet. Our climate plus our social, political, and economic customs have produced this characteristic American by the same biological process that characteristic Frenchmen, Germans, and Englishmen were molded from the same Aryan race-stream.

Our subjective moods are naturally being developed to meet the exigencies of our intensely concentrated mechanistic civilization. Our dignity is not pompous, nor are our profoundest feelings suppliant; our gayety is not graceful nor our humor whimsical. Our dignity lies in direct driving force; our deeper feelings are stark and reticent; our gayety is ribald and our humor ironic. These are moods which young indigenous American composers are born and surrounded with, and from these moods come a unique valuation of beauty and a different feeling for rhythm, melody, and form. It is precisely this spontaneous native feeling for distinctly different musical values which makes the problem of the serious American composer so especially difficult. His moods are not warmed-over moods of eighteenth- and nineteenth-century European society, nor is his musical material rearranged and retinted formulas of the standard classics

150]

which our audiences, teachers, and critics and our imported conductors and performers have been trained to think of as the only possible music.

To be more specific: Our rhythmic impulses are fundamentally different from the rhythmic impulses of Europeans; and from this unique rhythmic sense are generated different melodic and form values. Our sense of rhythm is less symmetrical than the European rhythmic sense. European musicians are trained to think of rhythm in its largest common denominator, while we are born with a feeling for its smallest units. That is why the jazz boys, chained to an unimaginative commercial routine which serves only crystallized symmetrical dance rhythms, are continually breaking out into superimposed rhythmic variations which were not written in the music. This asymmetrical balancing of rhythmic phrases is in our blood; it is not in the European blood. Anyone who has heard the contrast between a European dance orchestra and an American dance orchestra playing in the same dance hall cannot have failed to notice how monotonous the European orchestra sounds. The Hungarian and Spanish gypsies have a vital rhythmic sense, but it is much more conventional in its metric accents than the native American feeling for rhythm. When Ravel attempted to incorporate our rhythmic sense into his violin sonata, it sounded studied; it was studied, because he did not feel the rhythm in terms of musical phraseology. We do not employ unconventional rhythms as a sophistical gesture; we cannot avoid them. To cut them out of our music would be to gainsay the source of our spontaneous musical impulses. The rhythms come to us first as musical phraseology, and then we struggle to define them on paper. Our struggle is not to invent new rhythms and melodies and forms; our problem is to put down into translatable symbols and rhythms and consequent melodies and form those that assert themselves within us.

For instance: given a 4/4 meter, the European will generally think

$$\overset{1\ 2\ 3\ 4}{\text{♩♩♩♩}}\quad\text{(in quarters),}$$

or in eighths

$$\overset{1\ 2\ 3\ 4+5\ 6\ 7\ 8}{\text{♫♫♫♫}}$$

or in sixteenths

$$\overset{1\ 2\ 3\ 4\ +\ 5\ 6\ 7\ 8\ +\ 9\ 10\ 11\ 12\ +\ 13\ 14\ 15\ 16}{\text{♬♬♬♬}}$$

but the American is very apt to feel spontaneously

$$\overset{1\ +\ 2\ 3\ 4}{\text{♩–♩♩♩}}\quad\text{(in quarters)}$$

or in eighths

$$\overset{1\ 2\ 3+4\ 5+6\ 7\ 8}{\text{♫♫♫}}$$

or in sixteenths

$$\overset{1\ 2\ 3+4\ 5\ 6+7\ 8\ 9\ 10+11\ 12\ 13+14\ 15\ 16}{\text{♬♬♬♬♬}}$$

And moreover I repeat that the American does not think these rhythms out first as mathematical problems; they come as spontaneous musical ideas. Time and again I have heard my American associates play rhythmic - melodic phrases which sounded natural and spontaneous but which were very difficult to define on paper. In lecturing to groups I have repeatedly played rhythmic melodies before writing the melody. Invariably some musician in the audience will venture the comment that "it does not look as it sounds." Out of this unique rhythmic sense is developing a different feeling and taste for phrase balancing.

There is nothing strange about this American rhythmic talent. Children skip and walk that way—our conversation would be strained and monotonous without such rhythmic nuances, much like a child's first attempts at reading; nature abounds in these freer rhythms. The strange phenomenon is the power of repetition in accustoming our ears to the labored symmetrical rhythms which predominate in eighteenth- and nineteenth-century European music. Serious European composers have recognized for a long time that all the possible gamut of expression has been wrung out of conventional rhythms and the consequent melodies and form, but they were born with conventional rhythmic impulses, and when they write complicated rhythms they sound as they look on paper, i.e., unnatural. Stravinsky's "Les Noces," for example, sounds like an embroglio of rhythmic patterns. To quote Arthur Lourie, an authority on Stravinsky and his friend and champion: ". . . . Stravinsky's 'Les Noces' is so constructed as to prevent the hearing of the music itself. Here rhythm is driven to the maximum of its development and action; melody is totally submerged." Melody can be totally submerged by rhythmic action only when the rhythms are not an organic part of the melodic content and resulting form. His "Sacre du Printemps" changes its meter-signature so many times that it is extremely difficult to perform, but underneath it all is a steady reiteration of ultra - conventional rhythmic pulse. In fact the tympani player for the Los Angeles Philharmonic Orchestra told me that he rewrote his whole part into conventional meter-signatures. He could not have done that with an authentic American work in which the changing meter-signatures were necessary to the spontaneous musical phraseology.

American composers have not as yet developed any predominant type of harmonic idiom, but I have noticed two tendencies that are becoming increasingly prevalent both with our commercial jazz writers and with our more serious composers: (1) the avoidance of definite cadence which can be traced to our unsymmetrically balanced melodies (difficult to harmonize with prepared cadences) and our national aversion to anything final, our hope and search for more satisfying conclusions; (2) the use of modal harmony which probably comes from ennui of the worn-out conventions of the major and minor scales and our adventurous love of the exotic.

I am as confident that a national taste and talent for harmonic balance and nuance is developing as I am sure that we have already developed a national talent for unique rhythmic impulses and the spontaneous melodies and form which come from them. The American composer's problem is not one of inherent talent and authentic musical ideas; it is rather the problem of being assured adequate performances, receptive audiences, intelligent appraisals from commercial critics, and an unprejudiced analytic attitude from teachers and music schools.

The remainder of this article will be given to an exposition of the daily problems which the serious American composer must meet at the present point in our musical development.

The growth of musical culture is manifested in three

ways: (1) the understanding and discriminating appreciation of audiences; (2) the development of interpretative musicians; and (3) the production of characteristic native composition. Audiences are the roots of musical culture, interpretative musicians form the professional body of music, and original composition is the final fruit. And musical culture, that strange plant of civilization, develops in much the same way that a tree develops: roots, body, and fruit are interdependent. Obviously there can be no body of interpretative musicians until there is already an audience to feed it; nor can there be a growth in musical composition until composers have the necessary experience of hearing their works performed and appraised by capable and sympathetic interpretative musicians. Such musicians also relate the composer to his audience, and vice versa. Finally, audiences are dependent on interpreters and composers because they form the soil out of which audiences grow. Upon a natural and thorough assimilation of interpretative art and native creative art depends the growth and eventually the life of audiences.

So far American audiences have developed on imported music and imported interpreters. This does not mean that we are unmusical. It means simply that our people have been preoccupied with the building of our economic empire, that cultural pursuits were not pressing issues, and so we had to procure their products from nations which had already passed through the initial stage of civilization. As late as the time of Bach, German courts procured their music and their musicians from France and Italy. Only German church organists, choristers, and composers could grow on German soil, and it was not until the choral-variation forms grew

[155

out of the Lutheran church service that Germany really began to develop musically. Similarly American audiences will not grow into anything robust and wholehearted until out of the co-operation of native interpreters and native composers there grows some live, indigenous style and related form. This obviously cannot happen until American audiences recognize that they cannot develop very much more on imported music and interpreters. I do not propose a solution for this first and most important problem, but perhaps at least the issue may be clarified if we retrace the growth of this condition, step by step.

In the beginning it was natural and necessary that we import interpreters and with them their native music; and because America was conceived of as a democratic and capitalistic society, there was no court life; consequently music could be publicly presented only as an economic commodity. It was good business to import a musical personality and watch the eager, excited, socially exploited, and curious American dollars roll in. Barnum was the first big showman. He imported Jenny Lind, Ole Bull, Paderewski, and others. He plastered his artists with a thick coating of "hokum." Some he supplied with private bodyguards, others with superhuman attributes. He filled the newspapers with columns of "personality" stories. He auctioned off tickets for the "Swedish Nightingale"; he prospered and set a precedent. The practice of this precedent has been considerably toned down, but with the aid of subtle advertising technique and newspaper circulation it is even more widespread and more penetrating.

There came the development of reproducing machines—records and radio. Each invention has carried such an interest in sheer ingenious mechanical achievement that it has been possible and economically profitable to go through the same stages of musical development again. First in the concert halls, then with the reproducing records, and now with radio the America public has been and is still being led through the same imported musical literature and the same "personality hokum" about the European "maestro" interpreter. Like all good business men, the musical managers, companies, merger trusts, etc., have learned a lucrative formula which they will go on applying over and over again until box-office receipts indicate that it is no longer lucrative.

Then through the combined policies of managers, foreign conductors and performers, newspaper advertisers, commercial critics, music publishers and retailers, graphonola and record manufacturers and retailers, the devisers of the appreciation program in our public schools, and the professional music teachers and schools — the "great American public" has been very efficiently trained to know that it prefers an endless reiteration of the "standard classics"—meaning the best works of eighteenth- and nineteenth-century Europe, especially German instrumental music and Italian opera. The social significance of music is being smothered in commercial dickering, and all the crystallized procedure of incorporated business. Consequently the literature of music itself has become a vehicle for the performer instead of the performer being one of an infinite number of possible vehicles for the music.

This spreading lack of interest in musical literature and growing taste for gala performances and personalities is being understood and capitalized by managers, conductors, and performers. They are beginning to know we do not care

[157

very ~~much~~ what is presented (with the exception of modern works), but that it must be well performed and with the professional gesture. And our own cultural lethargy fits in well into the European cultural propaganda policy which is understood and accepted by all performers and conductors. For instance, Toscanini knew perfectly well that he would not antagonize American audiences or critics by touring Europe with the New York Philharmonic Orchestra without presenting one single American work. European critics commented on the irregularity of the proceeding, but our own critics accepted it as a matter of course. Toscanini also knew that he would not dare to appear in any European country without presenting works of native composers, and when Ravel publicly denounced him for his theatrical interpretation of "Bolero" he accepted the rebuke as graciously as possible. An American composer who publicly denounced Toscanini at his first 1930 concert in Carnegie Hall for his shameful neglect of American composition would have been cried down and probably jailed as a public nuisance. Until American audiences refuse to be browbeaten by conductors, performers, and critics, until we can accept fine performances and performers as the natural prerequisites of musical culture and become absorbed in the content and meaning of the music itself, American composers cannot hope for much support.

The professional body of interpreters divides naturally into participating interpreters (conductors, orchestral men, and soloists) and appraising interpreters (teachers and critics). Of the participating interpreters, conductors and their orchestras are by far the most important possible resource of native composers. In the first place, conductors and their orchestras have a closer and more stable relationship to the community which supports them. Touring virtuosi must master a few programs to mechanical perfection. If to this mechanical perfection they can add striking enough personality characteristics, their career is assured, provided it is supported by enough publicity management to maneuver them into the enviable position of being a box-office attraction. They simply tour all over the world repeating the same programs and employing the same publicity leads in each place in much the same way that a vaudeville act tours from one city to another.

Naturally such a touring virtuoso is very chary about including any modern works on his programs. His livelihood depends on steering the safest course from one musical port to the next, and he trims his sails accordingly. His hope is to ride on the popular wave of music which audiences know and unreservedly accept, not to arouse his audience to a critical attentiveness to the music itself.

On the other hand, conductors and their orchestras cannot afford to be too limited in their repertoire. They play to the same public each week for the whole season and their repertoires must be representative. So far the relationship of the American composer to American orchestras and their conductors is not a very fruitful one. In the first place, most of our conductors and orchestral men were born with European temperaments and were surrounded during their most receptive and plastic years with European musical traditions and idioms. They do not readily respond to our serious music. As a general rule they understand and prefer the commercial jazz idiom because it has a very steady rhythmic pulse, its harmonic texture is obvious, its form is elementary,

[159

its moods light, and its orchestration effective. Or if a professional gesture of social courtesy is unavoidable, the conductors generally program some American composer whose idiom and moods are frankly post-Wagnerian or post-Strauss or post-Debussy, one who has learned to capture some of the orchestral effectiveness of those composers.

But conductors do not like the emotional content of our more serious characteristic music; and above all they resent the technical difficulties of its rhythmic patterns and forms. It requires a new receptive approach in which neither the conductor nor his orchestra can rest on their experience. It requires conscientious work; it must be felt, and European conductors and orchestral men rarely have the time, the patience, or the desire to study our music thoroughly enough to feel it. They can play all the literature of the masters from memory; why should they sweat over a young American upstart? Let him get a reputation first! Consequently characteristic American works are side-stepped if possible, and if enough pressure is brought to bear to force their production they are very often given what is professionally known as a "scratch" performance. American audiences have been trained to appraise music by the mechanically perfect performances of Tschaikowsky, Brahms, César Franck, Wagner, Rimsky-Korsakoff, and contemporary Europeans, and they know that Bach and Beethoven are good regardless of performances; when they hear an American work poorly performed they conclude that the work was not good. They do not know that the brasses who were to outline the form of the middle section lost their place—and that all of the men were so uncertain of their entrances that they were afraid to give forth clear clean-cut phrases, that their tones were dull and muddy, and that, placed next to a standard work (which they could play with their eyes shut), the American work inevitably sounded dull and forlorn, faltering and uncertain.

This is an old, old story to many musicians and many patrons and friends of composers, but so far nothing has been done about it; and I believe this condition will not be radically changed until we have a new crop of young American conductors and orchestral men who were born with the American moods and American sense in their blood. Unfortunately the young Americans who thus far are being admitted into our major orchestras are so apt to be impressed with the honor of their opportunity and with the desirability of absorbing the traditions of the seasoned Europeans around them that they often become more rabidly prejudiced than the old routine men are.

This brings us to a consideration of the relationship of American composition to the big music schools and successful teachers. Naturally the objective of teachers and schools is the public success of their pupils, and their pupils are predominantly students preparing for public careers either as performers or as teachers. Prospective teachers must learn definite harmonic systems, definite contrapuntal methods, definite crystallized forms to sell again to pupils.

I recall a conversation with a very intelligent teacher who had frankly admitted that in composition each individual circumstance requires its own special solution, that consistency of procedure should be the only rule with respect to vital creative work; but when I criticized the teaching of definite crystallized rules to teachers I was answered somewhat as follows: "What can I do? These people come to me to learn something definite which they can teach to others for a living." This teaching of definite rules about harmony, counterpoint, and form, this academic emphasis on rules that have been culled from the most obvious formulas of obsolete styles is of course so much dead wood which must be burned out of young students' minds before they can have any intelligent understanding of the nature of American music.

One of the sorest problems which the serious American composers must face is the prevalent incompetence of commercial critics in appraising new works which they have never heard before. There are of course a few exceptions to the rule, but a first-rate critical faculty is as rare as first-rate creative talent and requires as much training. Most commercial critics accepted their positions as an escape from the wear and tear of the profession for which they prepared themselves. Some critics use their responsibility as an opportunity to work off their literary ambitions and naturally concentrate on literary phraseology rather than critical acumen. Very, very few critics were especially prepared in ear-training, musical analysis, and breadth of musical culture. Many of them probably admitted it frankly in the beginning, but their position demands the gesture of authority and they are so coddled by managers and professional artists that they soon lose that first perspective. It is much easier to learn to juggle words in the simulation of authority than it is to develop the authority itself. And even if they were especially gifted and trained to be competent critics, the commercial routine of having to write long articles on virtuosic interpretations of the same genre of music day after day, month after month, season after season, would dull their sensibilities. In fairness it must be added that even if they had the conscientious initiative to grow and keep abreast of contemporaneous output, their routine leaves no time or energy for growth. In Europe commercial critics are no problem because no one takes them seriously. Mahler even publicly invited them to stay away from his concerts and refused to give them tickets. But in America critics influence box-office receipts and consequently their ominous power is out of all proportion to their merit.

Finally, we must consider the fruit of musical culture in America. Is it going to mature? Can the flowering promise of so many talented American composers be pollinated by a genial and intelligent social interest in their native characteristic possibilities divorced from futile comparisons with familiar works of bygone eras? Most important of all, can American composers become socially and economically adjusted? It is my personal conviction that talented American composers will find an economic support more readily than they will achieve a social adjustment. There are many fellowships of recognition being offered for distinguished work. The John Simon Guggenheim Memorial, giving a stipend of $2,000 to $2,500 annually for two years; the Pulitzer prize of $1,500; the Prix de Rome, giving three years of economic leisure in Rome—these are some of the outstanding honorariums. (Unfortunately all three of the honorariums mentioned require the recipient to go abroad for his creative period.) But there is an increasing concern for the economic stability of composers. The Eastman School of Music and the Juillard Foundation are both publishing serious American works. Then there are the publication, *New Music*, edited by Henry Cowell, and the Cos Cob Press, of which Alma Wertheim is president.

The problem of social adjustment is a very difficult and many-sided one for the serious American composer. I have already shown that American compositions are not presented often enough or well enough to acquaint American audiences with American composers. This one condition alone makes the American composer remote. The prerequisite of all serious composers in all times has always been and will always be that of achieving a subjective calm sufficiently continuous and focused to enable spiritual and mental co-ordination. The solution of this problem depends on their finding and adjusting themselves to a congenial, stable environment in which they may develop slowly and naturally. This applies to a nature environment as well as a social environment. Man is so constituted that before he can profit from an intimate contact with nature he must first be at peace with himself, and this peace requires social adjustment. The man who seeks nature as a refuge from society can never absorb the pregnant silences which yield peace, reverence, aspiration, grandeur, and dignity. These moods are too impersonal and complete for the troubled man, they only mock him and send him back to serve his kind. Even if a socially unadjusted individual could temporarily achieve enough detachment to accept solace from nature, he must always in the end return to society to fulfill his destiny.

How to serve society as a composer, how to become economically and socially recognized as a worth-contributing citizen, how to establish durable human contacts with individuals or groups is a harassing problem. The shifting scenes of our social and economic environments are so fluctuating, so crowded with heterogeneous influences, such a helter-skelter race of commercial jockeying, that it is very difficult to strike any bedrock economic or human relationships. Our economic system has fostered the productive psychology with such narrow limitations that no allowance is made for the leisure which is necessary for productivity in the arts. Utility has become such a raucous slogan of our civilization that intellectual pursuits are generally socially appraised by the commercial value which they net from day to day. We have become so absorbed in material development that the intellectual and spiritual achievements by which all civilizations are eventually appraised are tolerated only if they serve an immediate commercial end. In this land of football, baseball, music revue, bridge, and motoring fans the social significance of music has not yet been realized or felt. In this land where athletes, air pilots, racing drivers, movie stars, and the sheer accumulation of raw buying-power are revered, it is difficult for a serious composer to avoid the devastating position of being elbowed by unschooled and thoughtless acquaintances into an apologetic attitude. The problem of social and economic adjustment is doing more to destroy talented American composers than any other problem, and of course its solution will come only when enough American individuals recognize that we cannot buy musical culture any more than we can buy a home environment. It must be believed in, cultivated, and used. Musical literature never has been and never will be valuable to society as a whole until it is created as an authentic and characteristic culture of and from the people it expresses. History reveals that the great music has been produced only by staunch individuals who sank their roots deeply into the social soil which they accepted as their own. After a musical literature has been created and traditionalized it becomes the common property of all civilizations. It is added to the cultural store of human experience as documentary evidence of the emotional gamut and intellectual skill of a people.

America is developing a distinctly different civilization from Europe, Asia, or the Orient, and our percentage of musical creativeness is high. There can be no question of stifling the ultimate musical expression of America. The only question which is under consideration is how soon we as a people will become intelligent enough to lend ourselves willingly and gracefully to the processes of time as they unfold our musical destiny.

> Will you seek afar off? You surely come back at last,
> In things best known to you finding the best,
>   or as good as the best,
> In folks nearest to you finding the sweetest,
>   strongest, lovingest;
> Happiness, knowledge, not in another place,
>   but this place—not for another hour but this hour.

The Music of Mexico

The music of Mexico is very diverse, quite as much so as are the racial, intellectual, and social conditions of the Mexicans. By far the best to do with the music of Mexico is to play it, or to hear it. But talking about it has also its interest. Very little has been written or said of the music of Mexico, and that little has been about some of its least important aspects. In this article I shall endeavor to make a general summary in more of a critical than an informative manner.

For many reasons the need of a critical review of the music and the other arts of Mexico is of utmost urgency. A knowledge of our history and of our country will make us really feel ourselves. The greater part of Mexican art has not really become completely Mexican, because Mexican artists have failed to saturate themselves with the life of Mexico in all the multiplicity of its expressions. Regionalism really becomes nationalism when nationalism comes to be in truth the balanced sum of all the regions. The "national style" will be the result of mutual understanding among the many groups of the Mexican people and of the country itself in all its manifestations. In Mexico not only does an almost complete gulf exist between the people of the country and those of the city, but even within the city itself there exist countless groups, more or less cultured, that do not know one another.

Tradition, in its best significance, should be considered as the substance of the conscience of a country throughout its

[167

past. Thus considered, tradition is a living fountain of knowledge and of character. There are peoples who have a well-established tradition. The Mexican people is not one of them. It has been impossible here in Mexico to sum up our life because the very factors have been kept apart by a multitude of political causes: The Spanish conquerors triumphed; as rulers in the land they governed, ignoring or denying the culture of the aboriginal element; at the advent of the Republic the racial, social, and intellectual conditions of the Mexicans had reached points of contrast violent in their degree of utter diversity, and to this day no form of proper co-ordination can be attained.

A revolutionary political organization, firmly established and fearlessly carried out, and a program which, bringing together all of the factors of Mexican culture, synthesizes one tradition will undoubtedly, in the end, give us nationality. Then we shall have culture and national arts. We talk much of "nationalism." Is this a symptom that Mexico is endeavoring to define her personality in all its varied aspects—in science, in art, in legislation?

The musicians of Mexico must know our tradition, for until such day as they do, our composers will not write Mexican music and they will go on saying that we have to continue in the European tradition and that the Mexican tradition does not exist. Professional musicians will continue their nine-year courses of composition, teaching our youth the rules of French and German conservatories. They will continue making us believe that music *is* Bach or Beethoven. They will go on destroying in our youth all its native force, annihilating all expression of the natural qualities peculiar to this race and to this country. Yet the Mexican painters of today have found the Mexican tradition of painting which the academies prior to the Revolution had denied without knowing.

A Mexican music exists. It is diverse, diverse in history and in the countless regional divisions of the country. But it has a character and vigor of its own. None of it but gives us fully the Mexican musical tradition. We may go directly to this music, in case it is the music played at the present time, or we may become acquainted with it by means of special investigations. The investigation in this case is not one of searching through cold, dead, archaeological material in an artificial manner, but rather that of identifying ourselves with the expressions of our own race, climate, and geography, from which, for absurd reasons, we have been temporarily disconnected.

The ancient culture of Mexico should in reality constitute a common bond among us; that is to say, it should be a factor which integrates our culture. The past, we now know, is as alive as the present, when the present is its natural consequence.

Factually, the music of Mexico may be divided into three great epochs in relation to our general history:

1. The aboriginal culture
2. The *mestizaje,* or phase representing the intermixing of Indian and Spanish
3. The nationalism of the revolution

The first epoch is known by a group so small as to be counted without difficulty; it is ignored by practically the entire public. But in point of force and originality this division is perhaps the most important of all.

Among the ancient Mexicans music was not only an individual expression indispensable to the life of the spirit but a concern of an entire state organization. Institutions for the teaching of music existed and special musical instruction was required in all religious and military schools. The political, social, and religious solemnities, as well as the various public celebrations of a secular character, always centered around music as a basis.

The sources of information about this early music are the chronicles of the conquerors, the accounts left by some of the ancient Indians who were educated, and the works of general history concerning Mexico which are recognized as credible; the knowledge of music possessed by the contemporary Indians who still, in many regions of the country, preserve the manner of execution and the forms of the most ancient traditions; and the study of the ancient instruments preserved in various museums of the world.

The second epoch is neither well known in its entirety nor in the various phases of its evolution. This epoch may be considered as extending from the Conquest down to the Revolution of 1910. It is rich in the variety of its manifestations, from the country and from the city, and includes the following:

*"Mestizo"** music from the country
    Sonnet (*son*)
    Ballad (*corrido*)
    Song (*canción*)
    Dance music—religious and profane
    Romance or pastoral (*pastorela*)

* Mixed Spanish and Indian.

"*Mestizo*" music of the city

    Compositions of the professional composers

    Concert and chamber music

    Dance music

The third epoch is the present. It may be considered to have begun when, in 1912, Manuel M. Ponce initiated the movement popularizing the Mexican song (*canción Mexicana*) and some of our regional dances, such as the *jarabe*. The very great interest which this movement aroused was undoubtedly due to the conviction of its initiator and to the nationalistic restlessness which at that time, and as a result of the Revolution of 1910, raged in a manner uncontrollable.

At the present time, with new phases of the Revolution begun in 1910 now lived through and past, leaving their very decisive contribution to the cementing of a criterion and a national culture, the musical nationalism of Mexico may definitely launch itself upon a determined course. It should consider itself as the product of balanced *mestizaje*, hybridism, in that the personal expression of the artist is absorbed neither by Europeanism nor by Mexican regionalism. We must recognize our own tradition, temporarily eclipsed. We should saturate ourselves with it, placing ourselves in personal contact with the manifestations of our land, native and mixed (*mestizos*), and this without disavowing the music of Europe, since it signifies human and universal culture, but receiving it in its multiple manifestations from the most remote antiquity, not through the medium of the "didacticism" of the German and French conservatories as has been our custom heretofore. We disdain the professional Mexican music prior to our own epoch, for it is not the fruit of the true Mexican tradition.

In the end we musicians must forge ourselves through work; we must make an art that is for all, not inclosed solely within the four walls of the concert hall. We must tend toward the more spectacular performances of music, theater and ballet, such as the ancient Mexicans were accustomed to enact, such as Greece had, spectacles which epitomize, which forge into one, the soul and the national conscience.

The Development of Cuban Music

Music, on account of its own inherent qualities, is far removed from the sordidness of everyday human existence. It is on this account a spiritual necessity, something essential to the flowering of all the better qualities of man. For this reason, if for no other, composers must devote themselves very seriously to the task of writing their best music. If they imitate other people's music, or already known styles, they are not expressing themselves, nor are they fulfilling their purpose of delivering an inner message to the outer world, through music.

I do not believe in the existence of good or bad, new or old, modern or antiquated music. All depends upon the quality of the message and its relation to beauty. If this message has the qualities of beauty and the substratum of genius it will be good, irrespective of the time in which it is written. New or old, it will be music. A divine or extra-human message delivered by human means—this is the eternal origin of all music.

In order, however, to arrive at a genuinely Cuban music, it is necessary to work with the living folklore. This should be polished until the crudities and exterior influences fall away; sane theoretical disciplines should be applied, and the music should be condensed into musical forms which shall be specially invented to be suitable, the same as has been done in the case of different European countries. When this is done, Cuban music will take its place with the music of the older peoples.

[173

Nothing could be farther from the line of Cuban musical progress than for its composers to drift into an imitation of current European tendencies. New forms, whether conservative or anarchistic, must be found into which to pour different ideas springing from native music. Such forms, however, are exterior matters; the inner meaning is of greater import. If this is of genuine value, the artist will have no trouble in finding the right concrete form for his abstract ideals.

So-called "Afro-Cuban" native music is our most original type of folk-song, and is a mixture of African primitive music with early Spanish influences. It employs many percussion instruments which have been developed in Cuba, and are to be found nowhere else, although they have their origin in African primitive instruments.

Referring to the employment of the peculiar Cuban instruments in symphonic works, I think that all of them might form part of the percussion ensemble of the modern orchestra; but as it is very difficult to have them in every orchestra, it would often be more convenient to obtain their sound and sonority equivalents with the percussion instruments of the normal orchestra, and leave the characteristic instruments for special use when they are essential to some particular composition.

The two native dance forms, "*danza*" and "*rumba*," both offer possibilities for symphonic development, particularly a new form of the *danza* upon which I am now working. Further forms will also naturally be invented. When these new forms, together with the new instruments or orchestral colors derived from them, are woven together into cohesive works which contain a genuine message, this message will represent the fulfillment of Cuban music.

The Artistic Position of the American Composer

The problem (of paramount importance for us) of the present artistic position of the American composer I shall endeavor to consider here.

Being myself an American composer [Cuban],* my aim is, of course, first of all to attain a production thoroughly American in its substance, entirely apart from the European art; an art that we can call ours, continental, worthy of being universally accepted not on account of its exotic qualities (our music up to now has been accepted in Europe mainly upon the basis of its outlandish flavor, that brought something interesting, something queerly new, being received with the accommodating smile with which grown people face a child's mischief, without giving to it any real importance); to produce a music capable of being accepted for its real significance, its intrinsic worth, for its meaning as a contribution of the New World to the universal art.

A new art—that is, new forms, or better, an American art expressed by American means, sensibility, form, ways— everything new and everything American, having its roots deep in a full and sincere artistic emotion. Modern, yes; but not with a modernity *"à outrance,"* not a musical expression *"pour épater le bourgeois,"* but sincerely felt and accurately translating the composer's emotions. Simple music may prove perfect, and highly superior in its expressiveness to

---

* When I refer to American music, musicians, or composers, I do not mean only the United States but use the term American in its broader sense, including North and South America as well as the Antilles.

the most imposing musical skyscraper built of superimposed quarter-tones.†

An honest endeavor should be made to study, to develop, and to make the folklore of our countries a living thing; not with the purpose of creating a local or naturalistic music, but aiming toward the universal, toward boundless art. For this the composer ought to have a thorough knowledge of our American means of expression and its possibilities, tending toward a greater and purer simplification of both the technique and the procedure; imitating nobody, not trying to compose in the manner of this or that master, living or dead, but in his own personal way. I have no faith in the sincerity or effectiveness of these returns to the style of a given composer that seem to be a fad in Europe lately. Old technique and old procedures do not match our generation's ideology and attitude toward life and art, especially that of American composers; we are offsprings of the old masters, but are far from them in both time and space.

A greater or smaller facility in creating music of the folklore type is not enough to indicate in an author the capability for higher enterprises that can endure the test of time. It is said that genius is self-sufficient, being the source of future learning. That is true, but nevertheless it is a fact, especially in music, that it is very rare to find real genius unaccompanied by a sound technical foundation, a foundation that allows the perfect development of the creative

† In my opinion, from a technical point of view, one of the greatest possibilities of music in the future lies in the development of the quarter-tone and the interpretation of music by mechanical means. Today their possibilities are as yet small, owing to their actual stage of imperfect development, which ties up the composer's expression. I think that an author cannot be sincere when he is entangled by the imperfection of his means of execution.

genius. Upon the basis of the thorough and sensible preparation referred to,‡ our efforts should tend toward constant attention to the contemporary movement in the artistic world, from the technical and the aesthetic point of view, and with the final aim of avoiding in our American art any attempt at Europeanization.

Indigenous instruments, both melodic and percussion, should be used, not in order to obtain an easy local color (something that I regard as not artistically serious), but with the purpose of widening their significance beyond the national boundaries. The sound of a banjo must not always bring jazz to our mind, nor should the rhythm of our *güiro* always recall a *rumba*. Those instruments of ours, speaking in a general and broad sense, are richer than the European ones from the standpoint of their sonority and rhythmic value, and ought to be mingled with them and sometimes take their place. Taking, as an example, some of the percussion instruments of Latin America, such as the *güiro* and the *clave* (in use in Mexico, South America, and the Antilles), we can state that their richness of sonority and their rhythmic precision have no possible equivalent or substitute among European instruments; and the same could be said referring to some others, like the marimba, the banjo, the *maracas,* and the drum in its different varieties.

As American musicians, we are in possession of a melodic and rhythmic basis as rich and varied as that of the original European countries. Let us create a continental art, and by means of developing our own American instruments present to the artistic world an art that is genuinely American.

‡ Unfortunately the majority of our composers, with a few noteworthy exceptions, do not possess this development.

American Tonal Speech

Manifestly one of the inborn traits of American genius is a sharp sense of technical perfection with a virile striving for it. This is the reason why the average technical provincialism of American music, often camouflaged by an up-to-date European tonal fashion, strikes me as strangely incongruous with the general American spiritual reach. However, to forge a truly expressive and virile technical medium for the American tonal speech would be, as mathematicians say, a condition necessary but not sufficient—not sufficient for a creative parity with other nations.

The American musical consciousness has yet to capture and to foster every individual spark, every creative breath that carries germs of racial and tonal America. We must watch with active sympathy and stress the germinal significance of such symptoms in the crystallization of a distinctive American music as the racial tenseness and exuberance of a Roy Harris, the New England mentality of a Charles Ives, a Sessions, or a Ruggles, the Western breeziness and hard color of an Arthur Shepherd, or the Eastern and metropolitan alertness and moodiness of a dyed-in-the-wool New Yorker like Louis Gruenberg.

In the past the growth of a distinct American music was hampered by an indiscriminate worship of European tonal tradition, but even more by the post-war contempt for musical culture and by a disbelief in its continuity. Jazz, for instance, did not acquire creative significance. It fell short of any rounded and full-blooded embodiment, because instead of ventilating tradition, fructifying and enriching it, jazz childishly attempted to take its place.

The new American composer, however, can escape the new demands of order, precision, and economy in tonal speech no more than he can tear himself away from the universal aesthetic basis of tonal art and the demands imposed by the continuity of musical culture.

Materials and Musical Creation

One cannot always regard different musical materials as distinct categories. Dynamic expression may be an integral part of a melody, or may be added to individual tones as an arbitrary embellishment. The border line between form and rhythm, in their commonly accepted sense, is often indistinct. In the subdividing of a phrase, who can say when the purely rhythmic figures begin? And is not the grouping of phrases (a formal consideration) the unfolding of a larger rhythm? Again, how is melody conceivable without rhythm and separable from it? However, admitting the conceptual differences between these terms, the element of form would seem to be the most basic of all, and inseparable from content, the other elements being often but aspects of form.

Personally I prefer that music, the most abstract of all the arts, be divorced from literary or dramatic connotations. In listening to program music, I find no pleasure in making the expected associations, although the music per se may give keen pleasure.

While I do not claim that the possibilities of the major, minor, and modal tonalities have been exhausted, I believe that the greatest music in this idiom has probably been written. On the other hand, specially invented tonalities, atonality, and polytonality open up vast fields as yet but little explored.

I find the present subdivision of the octave generally adequate for my own music, but I think that music would be tremendously enriched by other or more subdivisions. These would no more overthrow our present system than the *Tannhäuser* overture overthrows the music of Mozart.

Inasmuch as Bach experimented with his equally tempered scale, Chopin with "new-fangled" chords, Wagner with the valve horn, etc., I see no objection to present-day composers carrying on experiments of their own. Such experiments are typical of present developments in American music.

In the realm of aesthetics one guess is as good as another. My present theory of the creative act is as follows. It consists of four elements: the impulse or psychic urge which sets the mechanism in motion; talent (in the case of music, a number of specific talents); good taste, or aesthetic feeling, which now, as ever, eludes precise definition; and intellect, or the power of forming abstractions.

My musical ideas come intuitively, though generally only after a conscious seeking. At first they may seem satisfactory, even "inspired," but in the course of time often reveal shortcomings to an aroused critical sense, or properly speaking to a critical sense that for some unexplained reason functions well only after a lapse of time. In the many retouchings, complete rejections, and fresh beginnings which I find necessary, the three factors of talent ("inspiration"), aesthetic feeling, and purely objective reasoning work together, corroborating or contradicting one another. The final arbiter is aesthetic feeling, or a satisfied sense of fitness of the material, of balance between unity and variety, of the relation of the parts to one another and to the work as a whole.

[181

An Afro-American Composer's Point of View

Melody, in my opinion, is the most important musical element. After melody comes harmony; then form, rhythm, and dynamics. I prefer music that suggests a program to either pure or program music in the strict sense. I find mechanically produced music valuable as a means of study; but even at its best it fails to satisfy me completely. My greatest enjoyment in a musical performance comes through seeing as well as hearing the artist.

The exotic in music is certainly desirable. But if one loses sight of the conventional in seeking for strange effects, the results are almost certain to be so extreme as to confound the faculties of the listeners. Still, composers should never confine themselves to materials already invented, and I do not believe that any one tonality is of itself more significant than another.

I am unable to understand how one can rely solely on feeling when composing. The tongue can utter the letters of the alphabet, but it is the intellect alone that makes it possible to combine them so as to form words. Likewise a fragment of a musical composition may be conceived through inspiration or feeling, but its development lies altogether within the realm of intellect.

Colored people in America have natural and deep-rooted feeling for music, for melody, harmony, and rhythm. Our music possesses exoticism without straining for strangeness.

The natural practices in this music open up a new field which can be of value in larger musical works when constructed into organized form by a composer who, having the underlying feeling, develops it through his intellect.

Oriental Influence in American Music

All familiar musical terms, such as melody, harmony, rhythm, form, dynamics, and so forth, are capable of many totally different interpretations. There will be no "new music" unless the European interpretation is modified to fit the requirement of the new civilization-in-the-making. "Pure" music and "program" music are both fallacious terms and the products of a purely intellectual approach. All music is a tone experience. Music is to be heard, and what the tones produce in the hearer is the important thing, program or no program. Titles are at best sign-posts. "Exotic in music" is also a term which shows how narrow and provincial Western music is. All human music should be close to us, like all great *chefs-d'œuvre* of painting or architecture, irrespective of race or epoch.

Personally, I have used almost exclusively in my music so far what is so badly called atonality. Tonality, in the sense of "a principle of tone unity," is to me a requirement. But there are many possible "principles of unity"; when new ones are used, people, not understanding the new principle, consider that there is nothing but chaos. I believe absolutely in organic form in any art; but that does not mean in the least classical European formulas, or any one particular formula. I do not think anyone really invents a new tonality, unless it is an abortive product. But the evolution of a race-consciousness builds, era after era, new types of forms and a new sense of music, a new feeling of tone-unity.

I feel that anything that breaks down the narrow idolatry of musicians with regard to European musical concepts is valuable. The main thing to me is to change people's attitude toward music, to give to music a new and more vital meaning in the lives of men. To the extent to which smaller intervals will do that, to that extent I favor their use. I believe they will become necessary, but what is still more necessary is to realize melodic continuity between successive notes and do away with cut-and-dried keyboard scales. Oriental music can teach us that.

Composers should experiment with life, first. They should be great men and leaders of men. Technical experimentation is valuable today because we are in a period of transition. But in itself it has no permanent value.

If the composer had a profound and vital mind (and not merely an intellectual knowledge of technical mechanisms), his emotions then would surge from a depth of being which would preclude sentimentalism. "Intellectual grasp of materials" does not seem as important as a mental understanding of human life and of the problem confronting the human race. True creative power seems to me a combination of a profound, intense understanding of life and of a masterful control of emotions as well as technical means. The Orient could also show us the way by making us realize that the "culture of emotions" is the first step toward the development of a creative personality, especially where music is concerned.

The gateway to the Orient is through Occidental America. It is therefore natural to assume that it will be through America that the influence of Oriental music will first be felt in the Occident.

The Relation of Jazz to American Music

The great music of the past in other countries has always been built on folk-music. This is the strongest source of musical fecundity. America is no exception among the countries. The best music being written today is music which comes from folk-sources. It is not always recognized that America has folk-music; yet it really has not only one but many different folk-musics. It is a vast land, and different sorts of folk-music have sprung up in different parts, all having validity, and all being a possible foundation for development into an art-music. For this reason, I believe that it is possible for a number of distinctive styles to develop in America, all legitimately born of folk-song from different localities. Jazz, ragtime, Negro spirituals and blues, Southern mountain songs, country fiddling, and cowboy songs can all be employed in the creation of American art-music, and are actually used by many composers now. These composers are certain to produce something worth while if they have the innate feeling and talent to develop the rich material offered to them. There are also other composers who can be classed as legitimately American who do not make use of folk-music as a base, but who have personally, working in America, developed highly individualized styles and methods. Their new-found materials should be called American, just as an invention is called American if it is made by an American!

* As set down by Henry Cowell.

Jazz I regard as an American folk-music; not the only one, but a very powerful one which is probably in the blood and feeling of the American people more than any other style of folk-music. I believe that it can be made the basis of serious symphonic works of lasting value, in the hands of a composer with talent for both jazz and symphonic music.

Imitative Versus Creative Music in America

To apply the word creative to generally accepted musical compositions or newly evolved courses in musical composition is but to misapply the term, for the results obtained are not creative but purely imitative.

If it is true that all composers must learn their craft by imitation, we can find no objection to teaching the technic of composition provided it is based upon all of the musical systems, new and old. This is not the usual method of procedure. Almost all teachers, theorists, and composers ignore the importance of the Greek, Chinese, East Indian, modal, and all of the newly evolved scales, and have insisted for generations that the diatonic is *the* (and not *a*) system upon which the entire musical art must be based.

There are very few textbooks upon the subject of harmony, counterpoint, canon, or fugue that are not based upon the diatonic method. Many of them fail even to suggest the Greek and modal patterns in which the diatonic system has its roots. They are filled with rules regarding the formation of chords, the harmonization of melodies, etc., as the basis for creative work. It is never suggested that there may be other ways just as good, or perhaps better—many new harmonies, many new rhythms, many new intervals, infinitely many new ways of transforming the old into the new.

Examples from the great masters are given with the command that the student of musical composition pattern his work after them, which in the last analysis is but an insistence upon imitation. We find examples of the elementary subject of "accompanying patterns" (using a textbook term given) as the only accompanying figures possible, with the advice that the student make them a part of his musical resources so that he may use them in a practical way.

Sound pedagogy would say: "Here are the patterns invented so far; study them so that you will not use them. Find new accompanying figures for yourself. Study the works of the masters, but do not imitate them. Use their music for your inspiration, but do not copy it."

To do that which has not been done, to transform old material into new, to create new beauty, defining beauty in its broadest sense, to evolve something vitally new, built up sincerely and with an unshakable logic, is to be creative; to do otherwise is to be imitative.

I believe it is possible that one may have genius as an imitator. Would it be entirely wrong to say that Haydn had creative genius and that Mozart, who built his work upon the foundation laid by Haydn, had imitative genius? Few composers, however, have built a great art upon another's work.

When Bach in his early years wrote in the style of his Italian and German favorites he was imitative, but when he exhausted the possibilities of the material at hand and created his great fugues and the "Passion Music according to Saint Matthew" he was creative.

When Wagner wrote *Rienzi* he was imitative; but when he followed his own urge, when he exhausted the possibilities of the ninth chord, when he insisted upon developing new devices, when he wrote the opening bars of *Tristan und Isolde,* he was creative.

A composer may be creative only in a very limited way.

Ryebikoff discovered or invented the foundation for a new musical art, but it took another man, Debussy, to make use of all the new material in every possible way; and he left us work that is creative and not imitative.

Stravinsky in his "Rites of Spring" was vitally creative, but is he not imitative in his later piano concerto?

To follow the paths of any composer is but to be imitative. The modern and ultra-modern composers of America today have recognized this very definitely. They are developing a distinctively individual, new, and beautiful music. They rebel violently against any sort of imitation. They recognize the difference between imitative and creative music more than any other living group.

Charles E. Ives has created so much music that is beautiful and poetic, so much that is vitally strong and new, that he must be recognized as one of the outstanding creative artists of America.

Henry Cowell with his sensitive, poetic imagination and fine scientific approach, with his many discoveries, his tone-clusters, new rhythms, and other devices too numerous to mention, has added a new art to American music, and he is without question one of our finest creative artists.

Wallingford Riegger, a composer of fine attainments, who cannot be accused of lack of methodical training, must have recognized the dangers of imitating when he moved from the right to the extreme left. In no way disparaging his early compositions, I believe that his later works are more creative.

Adolph Weiss, Carl Ruggles, Ruth Crawford, and others have made important contributions to American music, because they are creators and not imitators.

Laws are made for imitators. Creators make laws.

Music and Its Future

To give the various instrumental parts of the orchestra in their intended relations is, at times, as conductors and players know, more difficult than it may seem to the casual listener. After a certain point it is a matter which seems to pass beyond the control of any conductor or player into the field of acoustics. In this connection, a distribution of instruments or group of instruments or an arrangement of them at varying distances from the audience is a matter of some interest; as is also the consideration as to the extent it may be advisable and practicable to devise plans in any combination of over two players so that the distance sounds shall travel from the sounding body to the listener's ear may be a favorable element in interpretation. It is difficult to reproduce the sounds and feeling that distance gives to sound wholly by reducing or increasing the number of instruments or by varying their intensities. A brass band playing *pianissimo* across the street is a different-sounding thing from the same band, playing the same piece *forte*, a block or so away. Experiments, even on a limited scale, as when a conductor separates a chorus from the orchestra or places a choir off the stage or in a remote part of the hall, seem to indicate that there are possibilities in this matter that may benefit the presentation of music, not only from the standpoint of clarifying the harmonic, rhythmic, thematic material, etc., but of bringing the inner content to a deeper realization (assuming, for argument's sake, that there is an inner content). Thoreau found a deeper import even in the symphonies of the Concord church bell when its sounds were rarefied through the distant air. "A melody, as it were, imported into the wilderness . . . . at a distance over the woods the sound acquires a certain vibratory hum as if the pine needles in the horizon were the strings of a harp which it swept . . . . a vibration of the universal lyre, just as the intervening atmosphere makes a distant ridge of earth interesting to the eye by the azure tint it imparts."

A horn over a lake gives a quality of sound and feeling that it is hard to produce in any other way. It has been asked if the radio might not help in this matter. But it functions in a different way. It has little of the ethereal quality. It is but a photographing process which seems only to hand over the foreground or parts of it in a clump.

The writer remembers hearing, when a boy, the music of a band in which the players were arranged in two or three groups around the town square. The main group in the bandstand at the center usually played the main themes, while the others, from the neighboring roofs and verandas, played the variations, refrains, and so forth. The piece remembered was a kind of paraphrase of "Jerusalem the Golden," a rather elaborate tone-poem for those days. The bandmaster told of a man who, living nearer the variations, insisted that they were the real music and it was more beautiful to hear the hymn come sifting through them than the other way around. Others, walking around the square, were surprised at the different and interesting effects they got as they changed position. It was said also that many thought the music lost in effect when the piece was played by the band all together, though, I think, the town vote was about even. The writer remembers, as a deep impression, the echo parts from the roofs played by a chorus of violins and voices.

Somewhat similar effects may be obtained indoors by partially inclosing the sounding body. For instance, in a piece of music which is based, on its rhythmic side, principally on a primary and wider rhythmic phrase and a secondary one of shorter span, played mostly simultaneously —the first by a grand piano in a larger room which opens into a smaller one in which there is an upright piano playing the secondary part—if the listener stands in the larger room about equidistant from both pianos but not in a direct line between them (the door between the rooms being partially closed), the contrasting rhythms will be more readily felt by the listener than if the pianos are in the same room. The foregoing suggests something in the way of listening that may have a bearing on the interpretation of certain kinds of music.

In the illustration described above, the listener may choose which of these two rhythms he wishes to hold in his mind as primal. If it is the shorter-spaced one and it is played after the longer has had prominence, and the listener stands in the room with the piano playing this, the music may react in a different way, not enough to change its character, but enough to show possibilities in this way of listening. As the eye, in looking at a view, may focus on the sky, clouds, or distant outlines, yet sense the color and form of the foreground, and then, by observing the foreground, may sense the distant outlines and color, so, in some similar way, the listener can choose to arrange in his mind the relation of the rhythmic, harmonic, and other material. In other words, in music the ear may play a rôle similar to the eye in the foregoing instance.

Some method similar to that of the inclosed parts of a pipe organ played by the choir or swell manuals might be adopted in some way for an orchestra. That similar plans, as suggested, have been tried by conductors and musicians is quite certain, but the writer knows only of the ways mentioned in the instances above.

When one tries to use an analogy between the arts as an illustration, especially of some technical matter, he is liable to get in wrong. But the general aim of the plans under discussion is to bring various parts of the music to the ear in their relation to each other, as the perspective of a picture brings each object to the eye. The distant hills, in a landscape, range upon range, merge at length into the horizon; and there may be something corresponding to this in the presentation of music. Music seems too often all foreground, even if played by a master of dynamics.

Among the physical difficulties to be encountered are those of retarded sounds that may affect the rhythmic plan unfavorably and of sounds that are canceled as far as some of the players are concerned, though the audience in general may better hear the various groups in their intended relationships. Another difficulty, probably less serious, is suggested by the occasional impression, in hearing sounds from a distance, that the pitch is changed to some extent. That pitch is not changed by the distance a sound travels unless the sounding body is moving at a high velocity is an axiom of acoustics; that is, the number of the vibrations of the fundamental is constant; but the effect does not always sound so—at least to the writer—perhaps because, as the overtones become less acute, the pitch seems to sag a little. There are also difficulties transcending those of acoustics. The cost of trial rehearsals, of duplicate players, and of locations or halls suitably arranged and acoustically favorable is very high nowadays.

The matter of placement is only one of the many things which, if properly examined, might strengthen the means and functions of interpretation, and so forth. The means to examine seem more lacking than the will to examine. Money may travel faster than sound in some directions, but not in the direction of musical experimentation or extension. If only one one-hundredth part of the funds that are expended in this country for the elaborate production of opera, spectacular or otherwise, or of the money invested in soft-headed movies with their music resultants, or in the manufacture of artless substitutes for the soul of man, putting many a true artist in straitened circumstances—if only a small part of these funds could be directed to more of the unsensational but important fields of musical activity, music in general would be the gainer.

Most of the research and other work of extending and distributing new premises, either by the presentation of new works or by other means, has been done by societies and individuals against trying obstacles. Organizations like the Pro-Musica Society, with its chapters throughout this and foreign countries, the League of Composers, the Friends of Music (in its work of uncovering neglected premises of the past), and similar societies in the cities of this and other countries, are working with little or no aid from the larger institutions and foundations which could well afford to help them in their cause. The same may be said of individual

workers—writers, lecturers, and artists who take upon themselves unremunerative subjects and unremunerative programs for the cause, or, at least, for one of the causes they
believe in; the pianist and teacher who, failing to interest
any of the larger piano companies in building a quarter-tone
piano for the sake of further study in that field, after a hard
day's work in the conservatory, takes off his coat and builds
the piano with his own hands; the self-effacing singing
teacher who, by her genius, character, and unconscious influence, puts a new note of radiance into the life of a shop-
girl; the open-minded editor of musical literature and the
courageous and unselfish editor of new music quarterlies
who choose their subject-matter with the commercial eye
closed.

Individual creative work is probably more harmed than
helped by artificial stimulants, such as contests, prizes, com-
missions, and subsidies; but some material aid in better or-
ganizing the medium through which the work is done and
through which it is interpreted will be of some benefit to
music as a whole.

In closing, and to go still farther afield, it may be suggested that in any music based to some extent on more than
one or two rhythmic, melodic, harmonic schemes, the hearer
has a rather active part to play. Conductors, players, and
composers (as a rule or at least some) do the best they can
and for that reason get more out of music and, incidentally,
more out of life, though, perhaps, not more in their pockets.
Many hearers do the same. But there is a type of auditor who
will not meet the performers halfway by projecting himself,
as it were, into the premises as best he can, and who will
furnish nothing more than a ticket and a receptive inertia

which may be induced by predilections or static ear habits, a condition perhaps accounting for the fact that some who consider themselves unmusical will get the "gist of" and sometimes get "all set up" by many modern pieces, which those who call themselves musical (this is not saying they're not)—probably because of long acquaintance solely with certain consonances, single tonalities, monorhythms, formal progressions, and structure—do not like. Some hearers of the latter type seem to require pretty constantly something, desirable at times, which may be called a kind of ear-easing, and under a limited prescription; if they get it, they put the music down as beautiful; if they don't get it, they put it down and out—to them it is bad, ugly, or "awful from beginning to end." It may or may not be all of this; but whatever its shortcomings, they are not those given by the man who does not listen to what he hears.

"Nature cannot be so easily disposed of," says Emerson. "All of the virtues are not final"—neither are the vices.

The hope of all music—of the future, of the past, to say nothing of the present—will not lie with the partialist who raves about an ultra-modern opera (if there is such a thing) but despises Schubert, or with the party man who viciously maintains the opposite assumption. Nor will it lie in any cult or any idiom or in any artist or any composer. "All things in their variety are of one essence and are limited only by themselves."

The future of music may not lie entirely with music itself, but rather in the way it encourages and extends, rather than limits, the aspirations and ideals of the people, in the way it makes itself a part with the finer things that humanity does and dreams of. Or to put it the other way around, what music

[197

is and is to be may lie somewhere in the belief of an unknown philosopher of half a century ago who said: "How can there be any bad music? All music is from heaven. If there is anything bad in it, I put it there—by my implications and limitations. Nature builds the mountains and meadows and man puts in the fences and labels." He may have been nearer right than we think.

BIOGRAPHICAL NOTES
AND INDEX

Biographical Notes

Here are included some biographical notes on composers who write or are written about in this book, together with lists of their principal works. For a more complete catalogue of the works of American composers see *American Composers*, compiled by Claire Reis, and published by the International Society for Contemporary Music, United States Section.

George Antheil

Born in Trenton, New Jersey, 1900, of Polish parents. Has lived in Europe most of his adult life, and has been the friend and associate of Igor Stravinsky and Ezra Pound. Guggenheim Fellow, 1932. His works have been performed by the Berlin Philharmonic Orchestra, the Frankfort State Opera, the Abbey Theatre of Dublin, the Stadtstheatres in Berlin and in Munich, the Concerts Golschmann in Paris, and in America.

Principal works:

1926. "Symphony in F," for orchestra	Universal Edition
1926. "Piano Concerto," with orchestra	Universal Edition
1928. "Second String Quartet"	Manuscript
1929. *Fighting the Waves*, for ballet	Manuscript
1929. *Transatlantique*, opera	Universal Edition
1930. "Capriccio," for orchestra	Universal Edition
1930. "Second Symphony," for orchestra	Universal Edition
1932. "Chamber Concerto," chamber ensemble	Manuscript

John J. Becker

Born in Henderson, Kentucky, in 1886. Studied in the Middle West. Author of articles on musical subjects. Founder of the

Contemporary Arts Society of Saint Paul, professor of music at Saint Thomas College and College of Saint Scholastica. Lecturer in numerous colleges. His works have been performed by the Pan-American Association in New York; and in Chicago, St. Paul, Columbus, and other cities, by other organizations and orchestras.

Principal works:

1928. "Symphonia Brevis," for orchestra   New Music Edition

1930. "Concerto Arabesque," for piano and orchestra   New Music Edition

1932. "Soundpiece, for Four Strings and Piano"   Manuscript

1932. "Dance Figure," stage work for singer, dancer, and orchestra   Manuscript

1932. "Symphony No. 2, Fantasia Tragica," performed at the Frankfort Music Festival, Germany

Henry Brant

Born in Montreal, Canada, in 1914. Studied in Montreal and in New York City, and is still continuing his studies. His works have been performed by the Pan-American Orchestra, by the Copland-Sessions concerts, and by the League of Composers, in New York. His piano works have been performed in Berlin and Dessau.

Principal works:

1930. "Variations," for four instruments   New Music Edition
1931. "Two Sarabandes," for piano   New Music Edition
1931. "Piece, for Eleven Flutes"   Manuscript
1931. "Sonata," for two pianos   Manuscript
1932. "Symphony," for orchestra   Manuscript
1932. "Burlesque," for eleven flutes   Manuscript
1932. "Concerto," double bass with orchestra   Manuscript

Alejandro Garcia Caturla

Born in Remedios, Cuba, March 7, 1906. Studied in Havana and with Nadia Boulanger in Paris. He lives in Remedios, where

202]

he devotes himself to composition and is also district judge. His works have been performed by the Philadelphia Symphony Orchestra with Leopold Stokowski conducting, by the Pan-American Association in New York, Paris, and Berlin, by the Havana Philharmonic Orchestra, and by smaller organizations and soloists in America and Europe.

Principal works:

1926.	"Two Cuban Dances," for orchestra	Edition Senart
1928.	"Bembe," for chamber combination	Edition Senart
1930.	"Three Cuban Dances," for orchestra	Edition Senart
1931.	"Rumba," for orchestra	Manuscript
1932.	"Yambo-O," for orchestra	Manuscript
1932.	"Suite," for eight instruments and piano	Manuscript

Theodore Ward Chandler

Born in Newport, Rhode Island, in 1902. Educated in America and Europe. Author of articles on musical subjects. Devotes his time to musical composition. His music has been performed in Paris by the Société Musicale Indépendente, and in New York by the League of Composers and the Copland-Sessions concerts.

Principal works:

1927.	"Sleep," mixed chorus a capella	Manuscript
1927.	"Sonata for Violin and Piano"	Manuscript

Carlos Chávez

Born in Mexico City in 1899. Studied in Paris, Berlin, and New York. His works have been performed in Mexico City, by various modern musical organizations in the United States, and his ballet was presented by the Philadelphia Opera Company with Leopold Stokowski conducting. He is at present director of the National Conservatory of Mexico and of the National Symphony Orchestra of Mexico, at Mexico City.

[203

Principal works:

1924. "Tres Exagonos," chamber ensemble   Manuscript
1924. "Three Sonatinas," for piano, 'cello, and violin   } Cos Cob Press and New Music Edition
1925. "Energia," chamber ensemble   Manuscript
1926. *The Four Suns,* ballet with orchestra   Manuscript
1928. "Piano Sonata"   New Music Edition
1929. "Sonata," for four horns   Manuscript
1931. *H.P., Dance of Men and Machines,* ballet with orchestra   } Manuscript

Aaron Copland

Born in New York City in 1900. Studied in Paris with Nadia Boulanger. Guggenheim Fellow, 1927–28. Founded the Copland-Sessions concerts for new music in New York City, and inaugurated the annual Yaddo festival of new music in Saratoga, New York. Has written many articles on contemporary musical issues. His music has been performed by leading orchestras and conductors throughout America and Europe.

Principal works:

1924. "Symphony for Organ and Orchestra"   Manuscript
1924. "First Symphony," for orchestra   Manuscript
1925. "A Dance Symphony," for orchestra   Manuscript
1925. "Music for the Theatre," small orchestra   } Universal Edition
1926. "Concerto," for piano and orchestra   Cos Cob Press
1928. "Two Pieces for String Quartet"   Cos Cob Press
1929. "Symphonic Ode," for orchestra   Cos Cob Press
1929. "Vitebsk," piano trio   Cos Cob Press
1930. "Variations," for piano   Manuscript
1932. "As It Fell upon a Day," voice and woodwind   } New Music Edition

Born in Menlo Park, California, in 1897. Studied in California and New York. Guggenheim Fellow, 1931.

Director of the New Music Edition, the New Music Society of California, the North American Section of the Pan-American Association of Composers, and the musical activities of the New School for Social Research.

Author of books and articles on modern musical subjects, lecturer on music in many universities. His works have been performed by the Berlin Philharmonic, the Orchestre Symphonique de Paris, the Budapest Symphony, the Philadelphia Symphony Orchestra, and numerous modern musical organizations in America and Europe.

Principal works:

1925.	"Ensemble," string quintet	Associated Music Publishers
1927.	"Some Music," for orchestra	Manuscript
1928.	"Sinfonietta," chamber orchestra	}Edition Adler
1929.	"Tiger," for piano	Russian State Edition
1929.	"Concerto," for piano and orchestra	}Edition Senart
1929.	"Concerto," for piano strings and chamber orchestra	}Manuscript
1930.	"Polyphonica," for chamber orchestra	}Manuscript
1931.	"Exultation," string orchestra	Edition Adler
1931.	"Synchrony," orchestra	Edition Adler
1932.	"Two Appositions," orchestra	Manuscript
1932.	"Rhythmicana," rhythmicon and orchestra	}Manuscript
1932.	"Four Continuations," for string orchestra	}Edition Adler

[205

Ruth Crawford

Born in East Liverpool, Ohio, in 1901. Studied in Chicago and New York. Guggenheim Fellow, 1930. Taught composition in the American Conservatory of Chicago. Her works have been performed by numerous modern music societies in New York, Chicago, Berlin, Hamburg, San Francisco, and other cities.

Principal works:

1925. "Five Preludes," for piano
1926. "Sonata," for violin and piano (four movements)
1926. "Suite," for small orchestra (two movements)
1927. "Suite," for five wind instruments and piano (four movements) } Manuscript
1928. "Four Preludes," for piano   New Music Edition
1929. "Five Songs," for contralto and piano (Sandburg)
1929. "Suite," for four strings and piano (four movements) } Manuscript
1930. "Four Diaphonic Suites"
    1. For two celli (three movements)
    2. For two clarinets (three movements)
    3. For solo flute (four movements)
    4. For 'cello and oboe (three movements)
1930. "Three Chants," for women's chorus
1931. "Piano Study in Mixed Accents"   New Music Edition
1931. "String Quartet" (four movements)   New Music Edition
1932. "Three Songs," for contralto, oboe, percussion, and piano, with or without orchestral ostinato (Sandburg)
    "Rat Riddles"
    "Prayers of Steel" } New Music Edition
    "In Tall Grass"

206]

George Gershwin

Born in New York City in 1898. Became known as a composer of jazz music and musical comedy hits. Later undertook the writing of more serious music, and studied in New York. Has, outside of his popular music, been performed by many leading symphonic organizations in America and abroad.

Principal works:

1923.	"Rhapsody in Blue," orchestra	Harms
1925.	"Concerto in F," orchestra	Harms
1928.	"An American in Paris," orchestra	{ New World Music Publishers
1931.	"Second Rhapsody," orchestra	{ New World Music Publishers

Howard Hanson

Born in Wahoo, Nebraska, in 1896. Studied in California and at Rome. Became professor of music at the College of the Pacific, later director of music of the Eastman School of Music at Rochester, New York. Has inaugurated regular series of concerts of American music in Rochester. His works have had performances by leading orchestras and other organizations in America, Amsterdam, London, and Rome.

Principal works:

1922.	"Nordic Symphony," orchestra	C. C. Birchard
1925.	*The Lament for Beowulf,* chorus with orchestra	} C. C. Birchard
1926.	"Pan and the Priest," orchestra	C. C. Birchard
1927.	"Heroic Elegy," chorus and orchestra	Manuscript
1930.	"Beat! Beat!" drums, voices, and orchestra	Manuscript
1930.	"Romantic Symphony No. 2," orchestra	Manuscript
1932.	*Merry Mount,* three-act opera	Manuscript

Roy Harris

Born in Oklahoma in 1898. Studied in California and Paris. Author of articles on musical subjects. Guggenheim Fellow, 1929. Has had performances with the Pan-American Association in Berlin, with orchestras in New York, Rochester, and Los Angeles, and with chamber organizations in many places.

Principal works:

1925. "Andante," for orchestra	Manuscript
1926. "Sonata," for piano	Cos Cob Press
1927. "Sextet," for strings, piano, and clarinet	Manuscript
1929. "String Quartet"	Manuscript
1929. "Symphony," for orchestra	Manuscript
1931. "Toccata," for orchestra	Manuscript
1931. "Andante," for string orchestra with clarinet and flute	Manuscript
1931. "Overture," for orchestra	Manuscript
1932. "Concert Piece," for orchestra	Manuscript
1932. "Sextet," for chamber combination	Manuscript

Charles Ives

Born in Danbury, Connecticut, in 1874. Studied at Yale University. Author of a book, and articles. Has worked almost exclusively in Connecticut and New York City. His works have been performed by the Pan-American Association in New York, Paris, Berlin, and Budapest, by Pro-Musica in New York, by the New Music Society in San Francisco, by the Havana Philharmonic Orchestra, and by various other smaller organizations and soloists.

*Principal works:**

1906. "Set," chamber orchestra	Manuscript
1908. "Violin and Piano Sonata"	Manuscript
1911. "Third Symphony," for orchestra	Manuscript

* The dates given here show the time of completion; many of these works were begun many years before the stated time.

1912. Three pieces for unison chorus and orchestra	} Manuscript
1913. "Holidays," set for orchestra	New Music Edition
1914. "Three Places in New England" (First Orchestral Set), for chamber orchestra	} Manuscript
1915. (Second Orchestral Set), for orchestra	Manuscript
1916. "Fourth Symphony," for orchestra	New Music Edition
1921. "Set," for chamber orchestra	New Music Edition
1921. *Lincoln,* chorus and orchestra	New Music Edition

Colin McPhee

Born in Toronto, Canada, in 1901. Educated in New York and Paris. Has made special studies of the folk-music of sailors, and of the music of Bali, where he spent a year. His music has been performed by orchestras of Baltimore, Boston, Toronto, New York, and Rochester; by the Scola Cantorum of New York, and by smaller organizations.

Principal works:

1927. "Sarabande," for orchestra	Manuscript
1928. "Concerto," for piano and wind octette	} New Music Edition
1929. "Sea Chanty Suite," for voices, pianos, and percussion	} Edwin F. Kalmus Edition
1930. "Symphony in One Movement," for orchestra	} Manuscript
1931. "Mechanical Principles," for orchestra	} Manuscript

Walter Piston

Born in Rockland, Maine, in 1894. Educated in New England and Europe. Lecturer at Harvard University and various New England colleges. His works have been performed by the Boston

[209

Symphony and Philadelphia Symphony orchestras, at the Copland-Sessions concerts in New York, and by the Société Musicale Indépendente in Paris.

Principal works:

1926. "Three Pieces for Clarinet, Flute, and
     Bassoon" } Manuscript
1927. "Symphonic Piece," for orchestra   Manuscript
1929. "Suite for Orchestra"   Manuscript
1931. "Symphony," for orchestra   Cos Cob Press

Wallingford Riegger

Born in Albany, Georgia, in 1885. Studied in Germany. Conducted in several German opera houses, and was conductor of the Bluetner Orchestra of Berlin for more than one season. He has been professor of music at Drake University, Cornell University, and at the Institute of Musical Art, New York. His works have been performed by Leopold Stokowski with the Philadelphia Symphony Orchestra and by Erich Kleiber with the New York Philharmonic Symphony, by the Pan-American Association in Europe, and by various modern musical societies in America.

Principal works:

1925. "Rhapsody," for orchestra   Manuscript
1927. "Study in Sonority," for ten violins   G. Schirmer
1930. "Prelude and Fugue," for orchestra   Manuscript
1932. "Canons for Four Woodwinds"   New Music Edition
1932. "Dichotomy," for chamber orchestra   New Music Edition

Amadeo Roldan

Born of Cuban parents in Paris, on July 12, 1900. Studied at the Madrid Conservatory, where he was awarded the first prize in musical theory in 1909 and the first prize in violin-playing in

1916. Moving to Havana, he founded the Chamber Music Society there in 1921. In 1924 he became concert-master of the Havana Philharmonic Orchestra; in 1932 he was appointed conductor of this orchestra. He is first violin of the Havana String Quartet, and the West Indies director of the Pan-American Association of Composers. His works have been performed by the Pan-American Association in New York, Paris, Berlin, and Budapest; by Conductor Sanjuan in the Havana Philharmonic Orchestra, the Mexican National Orchestra, and the Hollywood Bowl concerts, and by chamber organizations throughout America and Europe.

Principal works:

1923. "Fêtes Galantes," seven songs for voice
     and piano   } Verlaine

1925. "Obertura sobre Temas Cubanos," for
     orchestra

1926. "Tres Pequeños Poemas," for orchestra

1927–28. *La Rebambaramba,* Afro-Cuban ballet
     in one act

1928. *"La Rebambaramba,"* suite of five numbers of the ballet, for orchestra

1928. *Danza Negra,* poem for high voice and
     seven instruments   } J. F. Palos

1928. *"A Changó,"* Negro poem for Luths Quartet

1928. *"A Changó,"* transcription of the same
     piece for violin, viola, violoncello,
     and piano

1928–29. *El Milagro de Anaquillé,* choreographic
     Afro-Cuban mystery in one act

1929. "Dos Canciones Populares Cubanas," for
     violoncello and piano

1930. *Motivos de Son* ("Son" leitmotivs), eight
     songs for high voice and eleven in- } N. F. Giullén
     struments

1930. *Rítmicas,* I, II, III, and IV, for flute, oboe,
     clarinet, bassoon, horn, and piano

1930. *Ritmicas,* V and VI, for Cuban typical
           percussion instruments
1930. "Poema Negro," for string quartet
1931. "Tres Toques," for chamber orchestra
1931. *Curujey, "Son"* for choir, two pianos, and
           Cuban percussion
1932. "Mulato," for piano

Edward Royce

Born in Cambridge, Massachusetts, in 1886. Studied at Harvard University and at the Stern Conservatory in Berlin. He is the director of the Department of Musical Theory at the Eastman School of Music in Rochester, New York. His works have been performed there many times by the Rochester Philharmonic Orchestra. He has, besides his orchestral works, written much for organ and for piano.

Principal works:

1926. "The Fire-Bringers," for orchestra   Manuscript
1929. "Far Ocean," for orchestra   C. C. Birchard

Dane Rudhyar

Born in France in 1895. Educated in France. Came to America and has been naturalized for many years. Has written many books and articles on philosophical and musical subjects, and has founded the Hamsa Publications. Is a frequent free-lance lecturer in many colleges and other institutions. His works have been performed by the Orchestre Symphonique de Paris, by the New Music Society in Los Angeles, and by the Pan-American Association in New York.

Principal works:.

1921. "The Surge of Fire," chamber orchestra Manuscript
1923. "To the Real," for orchestra   Manuscript
1924. "Ouranos," for chamber orchestra   Manuscript

1928. "First Symphony," for orchestra	Manuscript
1928. "Five Stanzas," for string orchestra	Manuscript
1929. "Two Triphthongs," chamber ensemble	Manuscript
1930. "Hero Chants," for orchestra	Manuscript
1931. "Sinfonietta," for orchestra	New Music Edition

Carl Ruggles

Born in Marion, Massachusetts, in 1883. Educated in Boston. Conducted an orchestra in Winona for ten years, since when he has devoted himself exclusively to composition. His works have been performed by the Pan-American Association in Berlin with the Philharmonic Orchestra, in Paris, in Budapest, Vienna, Madrid, and New York; in San Francisco and Los Angeles by the New Music Society; in Venice by the International Society for Contemporary Music; and in New York by the Conductorless Orchestra and the International Composers' Guild.

Principal works:

1920. "Men and Angels," for orchestra	Curwen & Sons (second movement only)
1921. "Toys," voice with orchestra	Gray & Co.
1924. "Men and Mountains," for orchestra	New Music Edition
1925. "Vox Clamans in Deserto," for voice with chamber orchestra	Manuscript
1926–27. "Portals," for thirteen stringed instruments	New Music Edition
1932. "The Sun-Treader," for orchestra	New Music Edition

Carlos Salzedo

Born in France in 1885. Educated in Paris. Has lived in America for many years, and has become naturalized. Editor of *Eolus*. President of the National Association of Harpists. Professor of music at the Curtis Institute of Philadelphia. His works have been performed by nearly all the leading symphony orchestras of the United States, and in Paris by the Pan-American Association.

Principal works:

1918. "The Enchanted Isle," for orchestra	Manuscript
1922. "Sonata for Harp and Piano"	G. Schirmer
1926. "Concerto," for harp and seven wind instruments	} Manuscript
1928. "Pentacle," for two harps	Manuscript
1929. "Preamble et Jeux," for harp and chamber orchestra	} Manuscript

Lazare Saminsky

Born in Russia in 1883. Educated in Russia and other parts of Europe. Has been a citizen of the United States for many years. Is the musical director of the Temple Emanu-El of New York, the founder of the Polyhymnia Concerts, and an active officer in the League of Composers of New York. He has made special studies of the history of Hebrew music. His works have been performed by symphony orchestras in Amsterdam, Paris, Berlin, Vienna, Milan, Rome, and New York. His opera-ballet was performed by the League of Composers in New York, and in Vienna.

Principal works:

1914. "First Symphony—Of the Rivers," for orchestra	} Manuscript
1918. "Second Symphony—Of the Summits," for orchestra	} Edition Maurice Senart
1924. "Third Symphony—Of the Seas," for orchestra	} Universal Edition
1925. "Litanies of Women," voice with chamber ensemble	} Edition Maurice Senart
1925. *The Plague's Gagliarda,* opera-ballet in one act	} Edition Maurice Senart
1926. "Psalm 137," chorus, soloists, chamber ensemble	} Carl Fischer, Inc.
1927. "Fourth Symphony," for orchestra	Manuscript

1928. *Jephtha's Daughter*, opera-ballet in one act   } Manuscript

1929. *King Saul*, cantata   Manuscript

1930. "Fifth Symphony—Jerusalem," for orchestra   } Manuscript

Charles Seeger

Born in Paterson, New York, in 1887. Educated in New York and Europe, and at Harvard University. Head of music department, University of California, for seven years. Professor of musical theory, Institute of Musical Art, and New School for Social Research. Author of books and articles on music. Founder of New York Musicological Society, and editor of the American Library of Musicology. His works have been performed and staged at the Greek Theatre, Berkeley, California, and by soloists in other places.

Principal works:

1906–11. "Twenty-five Songs with Pianoforte Accompaniment"   } G. Schirmer

1908. "The Shadowy Waters" (after W. B. Yeats), overture for orchestra   } Manuscript

1912. "Three Choruses with Pianoforte Accompaniment"   } Manuscript

1912. (?) "Seven Songs," for voice and piano   G. Schirmer

1913. "String Quartet" (two movements)   Manuscript

1913. "Sonata," for violin and pianoforte (three movements)   } Manuscript

1915–32. Studies in single, unaccompanied melody and in two-line dissonant counterpoint   } Manuscript

1914. *Derdra*, pageant for orchestra and chorus   Manuscript

1915. *The Queen's Masque*, pageant for orchestra and chorus   } Manuscript

1915. "Parthenia," for orchestra   Manuscript

1917. (?) "Second Parthenia," for orchestra   Manuscript

1924 (?) "Solo for Clarinet"   Manuscript

Roger Sessions

Born in Brooklyn, New York, in 1896. Was educated in New England and Europe. Prix de Rome, Guggenheim Fellow, 1929. Also studied with Ernest Bloch in Cleveland. Has lived in Italy, France, and Germany for several years, and devotes himself to composition. His works have been performed by the Boston Symphony Orchestra under Serge Koussevitsky, and by orchestras in Geneva and Berlin under Ernest Ansermet. There have been other performances in New York, Cleveland, Rome, and Florence.

Principal works:

1923. *The Black Maskers,** for orchestra	Cos Cob Press
1926. "Three Choral Preludes for Organ"	Manuscript
1927. "Symphony," for orchestra	Cos Cob Press
1930. "Sonata for Piano"	Schott Edition
1932. "Concerto," for violin and orchestra	Manuscript
1932. "On the Beach at Fontana," voice	Joyce Book

Nicolas Slonimsky

Born in Russia in 1894. Educated in St. Petersburg. Came to America and has become an American citizen. Author of articles on music. Lecturer on music for educational institutions. Conductor and founder of the Chamber Orchestra of Boston. Guest conductor of leading orchestras abroad and in America. His works have been performed by pianists and singers in New York, Boston, San Francisco, Paris, Berlin, and many other cities.

Principal works:

1928. "Studies in Black and White," for piano	New Music Edition
1932. "A Game of Chess," for orchestra	Manuscript

William Grant Still

Born in Woodville, Mississippi, in 1895. Educated in the South and in New York City under Edgar Varèse. Has written successful popular as well as serious music, and devoted himself to composition. His works have been performed by orchestras in Frankfort, Germany, in Chicago, Rochester, and New York.

* *The Black Maskers* has been recently rearranged by the composer.

Principal works:

Year	Work	Publisher
1924.	"Darker America," for orchestra	Manuscript
1925.	"From the Journal of a Wanderer," for orchestra	} Manuscript
1926.	"From the Black Belt," chamber ensemble	Manuscript
1927.	"Log Cabin Ballads," chamber ensemble	Manuscript
1928.	"Puritan Epic," for orchestra	Manuscript
1928.	*La Guiablesse,* ballet with orchestra	Manuscript
1930.	"Africa," for orchestra	C. C. Birchard
1931.	"Afro-American Symphony," for orchestra	Manuscript

Edgar Varèse

Born in Paris in 1885. Educated in France and Germany. Lived in America for several years, and became an American citizen. Founded the International Composers' Guild of New York, and the Pan-American Association of Composers. Now lives in Paris, where he devotes himself to composition. His works have been performed by the Berlin Philharmonic, the Orchestre Symphonique de Paris, the Philadelphia Symphony Orchestra, and other orchestral organizations in Paris, New York, Boston, San Francisco, and other cities.

Principal works:

Year	Work	Publisher
1921.	"Amerique," for orchestra	Max Eschig
1922.	"Offrandes," soprano with chamber orchestra	Max Eschig
1923.	"Integrales," chamber orchestra	Max Eschig
1923.	"Octandre," for eight instruments	Max Eschig
1924.	"Hyperprism," for percussion and chamber orchestra	} Max Eschig
1927–28.	"Arcana," for orchestra	Max Eschig
1931.	"Ionization," for thirteen percussion players	Max Eschig and New Music Edition
1932.	"Metal," for soprano and orchestra	Max Eschig

Adolph Weiss

Born in Baltimore, Maryland, in 1891. Educated in Rochester, New York, and later studied with Arnold Schoenberg in Vienna and Berlin. Author of articles, and of many translations from the German, on musical subjects. Guggenheim Fellow, 1932. His works have been performed by the Berlin Philharmonic, the Conductorless Orchestra of New York, the Pan-American Association, the New Music Society of California, the Rochester Philharmonic, Pro-Musica, and the League of Composers.

Principal works:

1920. *Libation-Bearers,* for soloists, dancer, chorus, orchestra	Manuscript
1924. "I Segreti," for orchestra	Manuscript
1926. "Second String Quartet"	Manuscript
1928. *Kammersymphonie,* for ten instruments	Manuscript
1928. "Preludes," for piano	New Music Edition
1929. "American Life," for orchestra	New Music Edition
1929. "Third String Quartet"	Manuscript
1930. "Sonata da Camera," for viola and flute	New Music Edition
1931. "Variations for Orchestra"	Manuscript
1932. "Woodwind Quintet"	Manuscript
1932. "Seven Songs with String Quartet"	Manuscript
1932. "Sonata," for piano	Manuscript

Index

220]

Mexican composer, *see* Carlos Chávez

Mexican culture, 168, 169

Mexican tradition, 168, 171

Mexico, arts of, 167; Carlos Chávez on the music of, 167–172

"Modeling the line," 115

Monteverdi, 123

Moross, Jerome, 10

"Morte d'Arthur," by Colin McPhee, 37

Mozart, 78, 81, 181, 189

Music, in America, imitative versus creative, John J. Becker on, 188–190; appreciation of, 155, 157; attitude toward, 22; education, 22; and its future, Charles Ives on, 191–198; literature of, 157; Oriental influence, 185; percussion, 11, 46, 59; of the village church, 129, 130

"Music for the Theatre," by Aaron Copland, 53

Music Teachers' National Association of Schools of Music, 97

Musical culture, growth of, 154, 155; breadth of, 163

Musicology, 119, 124

"Nachtlied," by Adolph Weiss, 36

Negro themes, 8, 11, 217

Neo-classicism, 5, 6, 7, 20, 78, 114, 122

Neo-Romanticism, 22, 114

"New Fire, The," by Carlos Chávez, 103, 104

New Music, 62, 63, 163

New Musical Resources, by Henry Cowell, 59, 60

New School for Social Research, 60

New York Philharmonic Orchestra, 88, 158

"Nocturne," by Bernard Rogers, 88; by Gustave Frederic Soderlund, 90

"Nordic Symphony," by Howard Hanson, 98, 207

"North and West," by Howard Hanson, 98

Notation, 22, 59, 135, 136

"Octandre," by Varèse, 45

"Ode," by Aaron Copland, 50, 53, 54, 204

"Offrandes," by Edgar Varèse, 217

Orchestre Symphonique de Paris, 212

"Organ Concerto, The," by Howard Hanson, 98

Organ, outstanding composition, 88

Oriental music, 185

Ornstein, Leo, 4

Our American Music, vii

Overtones, 136

Palestrina, 30, 82

Pan-American Association of Composers, 63, 109

"Pan and the Priest," by Howard Hanson, 97, 98, 207

Parker, Horatio, 76

"Parthenia," by Charles Seeger, 121, 215

"Pastorale," by Bernard Rogers, 88

Patterns, 189

Percussion, 5, 11, 46, 112, 177, 211, 212; music of, by William Russell, 11; music for Cuban, 211, 212; with piano, 59, 104, 105; new sounds, by Varèse, 5; *see* Roldan

"Piano Concerto," by Colin McPhee, 37, 209

"Piano Preludes," by Adolph Weiss, 38

"Piano Sonata," by Carlos Chávez, 106, 204

"Piano Sonata," by Roy Harris, 68

"Pierrot Lunaire," by Schoenberg, 122

Piston, Walter, 9, 210; biography, 209–210; modernist, 126; Nicolas Slonimsky on, 125–127; works of, 210

Polychords, 123, 142

Polyharmony, 138, 142

"Polyphonica," by H.Cowell, 61, 205
Polyphony, 5, 10, 38, 66, 82, 95, 111, 134, 142
Polyrhythm, 80, 138
Polytonalists, 3
Polytonality, 58, 67, 79, 143, 180
Ponce, Manuel M., 171
"Portals," by Carl Ruggles, 14, 23, 24, 26, 27, 28, 29, 31, 34
Post-Wagnerian music, 9, 18, 160
"Prayers of Steel," by Ruth Crawford, 111–112, 206
"Prelude and Fugue," by Wallingford Riegger, 73, 210
"Prelude to Hamlet," by Bernard Rogers, 88
Prix de Rome, 90, 163
Pro-Musica Society, 195
Puccini, 8
Pulitzer prize, 163
"Putnam's Camp," by Charles E. Ives, 138

Quarter-tones, 11, 136

"Railway Train, The," by Adolph Weiss, 36
"Raising of Lazarus, The," by Bernard Rogers, 88, 89
"Rat Riddles," by Ruth Crawford, 110, 206
Ravel, 105, 151, 158
Redfield, Professor, 81
Reis, Claire, *American Composers of Today*, viii
"Rhapsody," by Wallingford Riegger, 210
Rhees, Rush, President, 86
Rhythm, and accent, 80; asymmetrical, 151, 153; characteristically American, 139, 151, 153; curious, 116, 121; different figures of, 47, 80, 134; of hymnsinging, 130, 134; importance of, 182; melody omitted for, 45, 47; original altered, 128; of sounds, 10; two at once, 137; use of, 112; variety, 116

Rhythm-polyphony, 142
Rhythmic impulses, American and European, 151
Rhythmic variations, 151
Rhythmical designations, duple system of, 59
Rhythmical phrases, five, 45
"Rhythmicana," by Henry Cowell, 60, 205
Rhythmicon, 60
Rhythms, analysis of, 47; chords of, 46; contrasting, 42, 67, 193; and cross-rhythms, 60; harmony of, 140; jazz, 138; new, 188, 190; parallel, 81
Riegger, Wallingford, 5, 190; biography, 210; on materials and musical creation, on Adolph Weiss and Colin McPhee, 36–42; Adolph Weiss on, 70–74; works of, 210
"Rites of Spring," by Stravinsky, 190
Rochester group of American composers, 85–92; concerts by, 97
Rogers, Bernard, 8, 88
Roldan, Amadeo, Cuban composer, 4; on the artistic position of the American composer, 175–177; biography and works, 210–212
"Romantic Symphony, The," by Howard Hanson, 97, 98, 207
Rosenfeld, Paul, *An Hour with American Composers*, viii, 52
Royce, Edward, 87–88; biography, 212; on Howard Hanson, 97–100; works of, 212
Rubenstein, 29
Rudhyar, Dane, 5, 110; biography, 212; on Oriental influence in American music, 184–185; works of, 212–213
Ruggles, Carl, 178, 190; biography, 213; Charles Seeger on, 14–35; works of, 213
Rumba, 174, 177
Russell, William, 11
Ryebikoff, 190